Prai[illegible]
TMI [illegible]

"From behind her shower door to her wide-open minivan door, as-seen-on-TV humorist Heather Davis riffs on the truly TMI of marriage and children."
— Ann Imig, *Stay-At-Home Humorist*

"Heather Smith Davis s so funny that if she were in my book club, we might not even need wine. Maybe. Davis invites you into her little corner of the heartland with heart and humor and a heaping portion of over sharing. How much information is too much for the Ultimate TMI Mom? Two words: drip dry. Even *I* wouldn't write about that."
— Lela Davidson, *Who Peed on My Yoga Mat*

"Heather Davis *would* tell if you if those pants made you look fat, then invite you out for cheesecake."
— Dani Stone, author of "Next Left"

Published by Buzz Books USA, an imprint of Athena Institute, LLC.

ISBN-13: 978-1-938493-08-9

Trade Paperback Edition

For bulk orders or to schedule an interview or speaking opportunity, contact buzzbooksusa@me.com.

TMI Mom

Oversharing My Life

Heather Davis

To Lauren -
Keep laughing!
Love,
Heather Davis

buzz books

Celebrating stories.

www.buzzbooksusa.com

For Brian who said, "Just do it." He wasn't always talking about my writing, but most of the time he was.

For The Daughters who, just by being themselves, provided me with enough material to write a book or two. And then some.

You grow up the day you have your first real laugh —at yourself. — Ethel Barrymore

Introduction

My husband* and I spent almost four frantic years trying to become parents. From the moment we became one in the eyes of the great state of Texas, we absolutely could not imagine our lives without precious little offspring who would have Brian's brawn and my brains. Those long years of trying to make a baby (which, to be honest, left my hubby with no complaints and actually made a few of his friends jealous at our required baby dancing) left me a lot of time to do a lot of thinking.

And by the time I was finally pregnant, I knew just about everything there was to know about being a momma. Hell! I'd been teaching teenagers for well over ten years at that point in time … it couldn't be that much different. In fact, I was so confident in my abilities as a maternal figure that I actually handed my doctor a birthing plan so that my precious baby could be born in a Utopian-like setting. The doctor thanked me by stripping my membranes. I do not recommend *that* little procedure unless you would like to feel like your insides are being shredded with a cheese grater. What? It's a real obstetric occurrence. Look it up. Well, the doctor doesn't use an *actual* cheese grater.

Unfortunately, something happened during the birth. As I was pushing that nine-pound, six-ounce baby out of what may be the world's smallest vagina (I'm still waiting to hear back from *Guinness World Records* on that one), I accidently pushed out all of my motherly-type knowledge, along with a gawd-awful amount of amniotic fluid, some poop and "just one little hemorrhoid," to quote the OB nurse.

When they handed me my beautiful newborn baby girl, tears welled in my eyes and I turned to my hubby and then to the nurse and finally to the doctor and quite possibly the janitor (I can't remember—the room was really, really crowded) and I finally blurted out, "What do I do now?!" Of course, every single one of them had their suggestions. With tears of joy (and gawd-awful fear) streaming down my cheeks, I turned to Brian and said, "Are you writing this down?"

We took home our beautiful baby and named her Daughter 1**. When our second baby arrived just two years later, she was honored with the name Daughter 2**. Nothing we read in the books made sense once we had the live specimens in our possession. Nothing that the parenting experts touted on television or radio held any truth with the actual fruit of our loins that we were now in charge of.

I remember sitting in a restaurant just two days before I became a parent and shook my head at the poor, pitiful, harried momma whose toddler was spewing cottage cheese from his smudged little mouth *a la* Linda Blair. I knew exactly what I would do should my sure-to-be perfect child ever behave in such a manner. I had my parenting plan in place even before I was an official parent. But now that I was holding my sure-to-be perfect baby girl? That spot-on parenting plan was as gone as Britney Spears' Mouseketeer reputation.

I guess my point is this: I was a professional wife before I got married. I was a professional mother before I actually became a momma. Life saw my cockiness, though, and began the barrage of lemon throwing. I had to provide my own tequila.

Now, on my best day, my mothering, my wifing (wife-ing? Who knows? I completely just made up that word I think) [For the record, yes, I did make up that word, according to my editor], my day-to-day living—those things are nothing more than amateur meanderings. My daughters? They are beautiful and smart and *professional* kids. I am not equipped to live this life. But I am equipped to laugh at every turn. And, my friends, there are lots of turns in my life. Boy oh boy, are there lots of turns.

Remember those asterisks back at the beginning? Yeah, here's where I explain them. Footnotes are so antiquated; let's call these "things-I-need-to-explain-but-don't-want-to-interrupt-my-groove" notes:

**My husband's name is Brian. He is also known as "Daddy," "Dad" and "Daaaaaaaaaaddddd." He would like for me to add that the words contained within this book are utter and complete heresy. I would like to add that he's not entirely innocent himself. Nor is he worthy of a name change.*

***Daughter 1's and Daughter 2's ~~names have been changed to protect the innocent~~. ~~names have been changed to grant them some anonymity~~. ~~names have been changed to keep them out of therapy~~. names have been changed to lessen the time they spend in therapy.*

Close enough.

My Bladder Is Out To Get Me Or The Story Overshared on National Television

I thrive on routine, especially in the mornings. If I didn't have a routine in the mornings, I would never get anywhere I needed to be and would never get anything done. So, unless I'm on a vacation or visiting somewhere, I adore and adhere to my routines. The sun rises and sets on my routines.

This particular week, however, really drove home the point that I am almost (not entirely) too dependent on my routines.

Let us start from the beginning.

The alarm went off and I hit the snooze seven times. This, my friends, is the only time in my life where I actually use math. I figure the latest I can get up, then I figure backwards the number of times I can hit snooze and not be completely off schedule.

I got up and brushed my teeth. I do this first thing. This gives me just a smidgen of a chance more to wake up (as if the seven snoozes weren't enough).

Then I took my shower. Here's where the multi-tasking starts. Because I love you so much, I'm choosing to confess this to you right here, right now. I pee in the shower. Oh, c'mon! I'm willing to bet that about half of you do it as well. And about forty-seven percent of you are lying about not peeing in the shower.

I find many things in my life disgusting. Peeing in the shower is not one of them. Brian happens to be one of those three percent who don't pee in the shower, and he is one of those who happen to find it disgusting. But, as the old saying goes, "Those who blow their nose in the shower shouldn't throw toilet paper at those who pee." Am I right?

Anyhoo, back to routines.

After I shower and pee, I put in my contacts, do my face, lotion up my body, get dressed, do my hair and I'm ready to roll-all in under thirty minutes. I'm convinced that peeing in the shower really does save that much time.

This routine is sure-fire, never-fail success in the morning for me. I could do this routine in my sleep. And I have on many, many, many occasions. It's a routine that is engrained in my being, and I don't begrudge that one bit.

So, this day, we had errands to run. I went through my morning routine and got The Daughters up and going and we headed out the door only to discover that the gas gauge in the van is sitting on empty; we're racing on fumes to the gas station, where through a silly series of events involving two overly-helpful Daughters, I end up with gasoline all over my feet.

Not a problem! I can roll with minor setbacks. I have routines in place just for this exact reason. I'll just run home, rinse off my feet, change shoes and we'll be right back on target, no?

Maybe.

We race back home, and I leave The Daughters in the van. One Direction was on the radio; they wouldn't have heard me if I'd screamed through a bullhorn that we were going to Disney World.

I considered going to the back yard to just rinse off

with the hose. But, it had been raining and our dumb dog Bo would have jumped on me and gotten me dirty and I would have had to shower and get ready all over again! How's that for forward thinking? How's that for proactive, problem solving? I had a plan and as soon as I rinsed off, I could get right back to it.

So, I went into the bathroom, turned on the shower, stepped in toward the back so I could just rinse my feet off and promptly settled into my morning routine.

Yes, that's right, my friends, I peed my pants.

Read it again if you need to.

Laugh at me if you will.

But I admit it. I peed my pants.

Immediately, I thought, "Oh. My. Goodness." No, I actually thought, "What the hell?"

Then I promptly, as is my routine, turned my back to the faucet and wet my hair down.

Yes. Your assumptions are correct. I am standing fully clothed-in the shower, going through my shower routine. At this realization, I thought, "Well, shit."

Ya know? Sometimes it just stands to reason that you go with the flow. In this case, the shower-flow. I disrobed, continuing with my morning routine. And I made it back to the minivan in a record-breaking fourteen minutes, just as One Direction was assuring my tweens that they were beautiful.

The Daughters were still entranced. And didn't even notice the wet ponytail or the new clothes.

Hot And Spicy Momma

I'm a pretty good cook. And I'm actually a great cook—about once a month.

See, once a month, Brian hosts a poker game. I call it The Bro Date much to the great enjoyment of Brian—NOT. At The Bro Date, he and four or so of his little buddies hang out, eat, drink and play cards. On occasion (once) I caught them watching a movie. It was a documentary about Okie Noodling, or, for those of you with an ounce of culture in your system, fishing for catfish in muddy waters with nothing but your hands. I am not kidding. They were not watching sports or porn; they were watching stupidity. On evenings where they are a bit looser with their cards, they'll watch Shake Weight infomercials. I'm not sure whether this makes me laugh or cry.

To prepare for The Bro Date, I spend all day Saturday cleaning the house. Not that the Broes (Bro's?) will notice, but in case they decide to go home to their wives and discuss the cleanliness of my home, I want it to be a good discussion. It would actually be a lively discussion with lots of laughter and snorting because I know all the wives and they will know that I had spent all day cleaning because my house is—otherwise—never party-worthy.

Additionally, I make fun food! In fact, all the wives do. There's always a sub sandwich and nacho dip, of course—staples of poker games the world over. And then there are those wives who erroneously think like me:

They believe that the boys sit around discussing the recipes their wives used to make them their delightful snacks. We are wrong, of course, because it's hard to discuss food when your mouth is stuffed with it. The only reason I know what the other Broes bring (Bro's looks better, but is grammatically wrong, I'm pretty sure.) [Note from my editor: *Let's go with Bros. Both Broes and Bro's make me twitchy.*] (Note from me: *There ya go.*) The only reason I know what the other Bros bring is that I analyze the plates on Sunday morning to try and figure out what they have eaten. I take in the smells left over in my sink and begin planning my choice for the next month so that I can one-up the other wives. No. I didn't just say that. What I meant was I want to plan ahead a thoughtful dish that will be appealing to all.

Then, I quiz Brian until he gives me the full-blown exact menu.

Finally, I decide what I'm going to make the next month so that I am still the reigning Food-Diva and all the Bro's (screw grammar) [Note from my editor: *No we will not screw grammar.*] (Note from me: *So, yeah.*) *Bros* will hail my cooking as supreme among women. Of course, I know this won't happen, but a girl's gotta dream (of bratwurst wrapped in chipotle cheddar).

What I have learned is that I can add jalapeños to almost anything and it's gonna get eaten. Including pancakes—oh yes it will be eaten. Trust me on that one.

What another wife has learned, she shared with me after I bragged about my latest Food Network-worthy endeavor, is that she can throw cheese on top of anything—including week-old taco meat, send it to The

Bro Date and the dish will come back empty … I'm not sure what she's trying to tell me here …

For the most recent Bro Date, I bought some fresh jalapeños to mix with sausage, cheese and Bisquick (secret family recipe—or ancient Chinese secret, either way). I chopped up three of those fabulously hot peppers—and promptly got a tickle up my nose. I dashed into the bathroom just off the kitchen, grabbed some toilet paper and blew my nose.

Immediately, my nose and eyes began to water … Uh-huh. I had just pepper-burned my nostrils when the jalapeño "juice" from my hands transferred to the toilet paper. In the midst of this sneezing fit, coupled with my runaway nose I had to go to the bathroom. You know, urinate. I would have said that I had to PEE, but my mother and my mother-in-law will be reading this, and I don't want to horrify them. Quickly, I took my seat—my eyes watering to beat all, my nose burning like Chicago after Mrs. O'Leary's cow went to town, and I'm sneezing like a mad woman. I grabbed more toilet paper waded it up and used it as the manufacturers intended it be used: I wiped myself.

And all of a sudden, I'm the new spice girl.

I am in the hot seat.

I'm a hunka, hunka burnin' love.

My loins belong in a Harlequin novel.

I felt, literally, like I was in heat. *Literally*.

It was not pretty, my friends.

When one's mouth is on fire from peppers, one eats bread. I did learn that from my good friend, Rachael—you know, Rachael Ray. But, to be honest, all I could think of was that if I applied bread to this region, I'm pretty sure I'd end up with a yeast infection. And to be honest, at this point, a full-blown yeast infection would have been a welcome relief.

Never fear, (of course, you're not fearing, your woo-woo was not wired with fire), I quickly found some sort of topical ointment that we had in the medicine closet (after I came to with the help of Brian and some smelling salts). I finished my snack for the Bro Date then I retreated to the bedroom—where I placed an ice pack on my eyes, on my nose and, well, pretty much every other orifice I have.

Next month, The Bros are getting Oreos. If I'm feeling particularly saucy, I'll buy the Double Stuffed … or the Mint Oreos … Then crush them into ice cream, mix it up, form it into balls and roll them in jalapeños … How quickly I forget.

It's Shake And Bake And No One Helped

While waiting for my interpretive dancing daughters to get out of Basic Ballet class—yes, I realize that it's a waste of money to give dance lessons to interpretive dancers, *now*—I overheard some dance mommas gossiping (I mean chatting) about this great new place that allowed them to be June Cleaver. Through their raves and revelations, I was introduced to a little slice of heaven known as Delightful Dinners. I visited once and became a fan.

Delightful Dinners was this fun little place where I would escape once a month and prepare scrumptious meals for my lovely family. The way this marvel of the modern culinary world worked was that I would go to their store and they would have ingredients for several meals set up at various stations around their extremely large and very cool-looking kitchen. I would "create" the meals, pay my penance, take them to my humble abode to my awaiting freezer and bake them when dinnertime rolled around. What made this place heaven was that they did all the prep work. All I had to do was show up, assemble the meal, drink a little sangria and go home feeling very much like the homemaker I was not. And, I didn't have to clean up. Bonus! The utensils and prep area seemed to clean themselves.

I loved my little food assembly escape. I would pretend to be Rachael Ray, hosting my own TV show. With a bit more sangria than usual, I would actually talk to my pretend studio audience. Okay. This only happened once and they called Brian to come and get me. No one was harmed in the making of that Salisbury steak. Also, because I am an outside-my-home working momma, I would go after work and by the time I got home The Daughters would already be bathed, brushed and sound asleep. It was my little once-a-month vacation.

I would cheerfully select my "menu" each month and decide which twelve meals I would lovingly prepare for my family. I would always split the meals, thus bringing home between twenty and twenty-four meals. Then I'd pile them into the freezer and get one out each morning to defrost. Cook it that evening, throw away the disposable containers and call myself Martha Stewart. Lately, I have been getting greyer than I like, so I should start calling myself Paula Deen. After all, I do sound more southern than northeastern.

It was a lifesaver for me in the evenings as The Daughters learned quickly how to cook the frozen meals themselves, leaving me time to catch up on my DVR'd *Duck Dynasty*. I kid; I kid. I'd help the girls get the oven turned to the correct temperature first, of course.

I am sad to say (excuse me while I compose myself), my meal assembly place closed their doors. (Sob!) When I heard the news I quickly called up the owner (whom I'd become quite close to since she'd saved my sanity through food preparation) and said, "What the hell!??!" How totally inconvenient for her and her husband to move when clearly, I still had mouths to feed at my house. "What am I supposed to do now? *Cook*?" When the phone clicked, I realized that we weren't quite as close as I had thought.

Since I had run out of freezer meals, I sat down with Brian and The Daughters to make a list of what they really liked to eat. My plan was to go to the store, get groceries for the month and create Delightful Dinners in my own little kitchen.

The very first recipe I looked up was one for homemade sangria.

The list was really very helpful. The Daughters and The Dad were very clear in their desires, and it made my list very concise: macaroni, cheese, and steak.

I made the sangria first.

The first Saturday after my freezer was looking really bare, I carefully charted a month-long menu and set out to the grocery store. I came home, played some old school disco on the stereo and mentally and physically prepared to cook. Really, it wasn't as tough as I anticipated. I chopped and diced and sliced first and made my own assembly line. I grabbed my baggies and began filling. I tossed some salt and pepper in, shook the bag and placed it in the freezer. Wow! Two meals down.

I was feeling all kinds of empowered. I began calling myself Rachael and I didn't care who heard me talking to my pretend-studio audience. Actually, Brian and The Daughters were out hitting golf balls, so if anyone heard me talking to myself, they shouldn't have been in our house to begin with and maybe my seemingly diminished mental capacity would have encouraged them to go right back out of our house.

I was making my own version of meal-prep look like I'd been doing it my whole life! And then the tetrazzini … hit the floor. I was getting a little bit showboat-y and forgot to seal the baggie before I began shaking the baggie. It was Okay; I was still good. I cleaned up the creamy Italian goodness and moved on to Mexican lasagna. It was my hope to expose my family to all cultures of food. Except Indian food or anything else made with curry—I hate to clean toilets. [Note from my editor: *Eww*!]

Mexican Lasagna. Step one: Drain the corn and the beans. And as I dumped them into the sink, I remembered one very important rule about draining cans of things. Make sure there's something to drain them with.

Such as a colander.

Which I had *not* placed in the sink.

Hey, no big deal! I'll just move right on to the stuffed peppers. Where were those peppers? Right. I diced them all in my dicing mania earlier. Fine. We'll turn it into meatloaf—just grab the ground beef from the fridge. Ground beef. Ground beef. Ground beef. How in the world could I not have bought ground beef? Oh. Wait. It's frozen. As in solid, and still in the freezer.

I had made a total of three of my eighteen planned meals before my culinary juices were all dried up. When Brian and The Daughters got home from the golf course, they stopped on their way through the garage to check out the freezer, which was for all intents and purposes, still empty. They came, cautiously, into the kitchen and found me sitting at the table with the phone in one hand, a pen in the other, a half-empty pitcher of sangria on the placemat before me and a pile of dishes and utensils in the sink because apparently they don't clean themselves.

Brian, because he's a smart one, commented first: "Honey! It sure smells delish in here!"

The Daughters, because they are inquisitive, questioned me: “Whatcha doing with that calendar, Momma?”

Me, because I am a brave enough woman to admit defeat: “I’m making a list of what restaurants let kids eat free on what days.”

At least I learned how to make sangria on my own. I found out that sangria really did make me feel like a better cook! At least it made me feel not so guilty about quesadillas five times a week.

Open Up! It's The Police!

The first Valentine's Day my husband and I spent as a married couple found me without a voice. Seriously, I had laryngitis. I couldn't have talked if I had been handed a mic and a live audience.

Shhh … Do you hear that? All the other Dads out there are saying, "Wow! How'd he score that??!? No nagging about the lack of flowers and chocolate. *A DAY OF SILENCE FROM HIS WIFE!*? He's one lucky man!"

And let me just stop that particular little story right there and say, "Hardy-har-har."

Let me also say that my hubby is not a traditional Valentine's Day gift-giver. From the day we began dating, he made it clear that he did not give into the commercialism of V-day. He would send me flowers for other occasions, just not Valentine's Day.

He was completely romantic in many other ways, though. After we'd been dating for one month, I got one single yellow rose. On our two-month dating anniversary, I got two yellow roses. When our third-month dating anniversary rolled around, I got three yellow roses. You get the picture, right?

Once we were engaged, I got a roses and a chocolate-truffle countdown calendar to our wedding day. So stinkin' sweet.

We are both educators, and over our spring break, we eloped. It was a sweet ceremony with only our immediate family in attendance. We ate our first matrimonial meal at a catfish-slash-BBQ joint and stayed our first night at a Motel 6. Did you not hear me? We're teachers. Motel 6 was living it up.

On the day I returned to my classroom, after we were married, I got a dozen yellow roses and a card that read, "I just want you to know that these won't stop coming just because you've married me."

And I haven't gotten flowers since.

Okay—that's not true. Once, we were out to lunch with friends and I told them that he hadn't sent me flowers after making that promise and he sent me flowers the very next day. He also emailed my friends to let them know he did it. And just last month, when I was bragging about a friend's husband who had gotten her a NEW PHONE and one who had got her tickets to NORAH JONES, he sent me flowers just to maintain his spot in "The Good Husband Notebook" that my friends and I maintain. (Not really. That's not true. We don't have a notebook. It's a blog.)

I don't tell you all this so you'll think, "Oh! Poor Momma! What a dork she's married to!" He does so many other really nice things for me in the meantime that I really have no complains. But, rest assured, he is pretty much a very nice dork.

I mean, c'mon, when I holler that I need some toilet paper, he always brings me to two rolls. Really!

And one time, he had our daughters tell me to stay in bed because breakfast was coming. And an hour later—after they had eaten—I got a cold egg sandwich, once they remembered I was still in bed. It's the thought that counts, right?

He has sat through the stage version of *Mamma Mia!* not once, not twice, but three times! And he's only fallen asleep twice! The third time, I purposefully sang along loud enough to keep him awake. And then after the usher—or rather the *husher*—told me to be quiet, he stayed awake for fear of being escorted out. What a chicken.

He lets me warm my cold feet on the back of his knees. He makes me popcorn and adds extra butter just for my bowl. He matches the socks—well, "matches" isn't the right word—he *folds* the socks. He warms up my van in the morning. AND (this one's a biggie!) he knows where I hide my stash of Cool Mint Oreos and he doesn't sneak any. He's a great guy.

Let's return to the original story: Our first Valentine's Day as a married couple … I woke up without a voice. I couldn't even mutter, "I can't talk!" Brian, who drove a bus in addition to teaching and coaching at the time, left our apartment an hour before I did. I would usually wake up enough to go to the bathroom and kiss him goodbye, then I'd hit the snooze button six more times.

On this particular Valentine's morning, when Brian came back into the apartment after starting his truck, I wrote out a note asking him to call in for me since I couldn't talk.

Right after he called in sick for me, he called in sick for himself. Of course, he was *love* sick, but sick days are sick days. We were newlyweds still, for goodness sake. [Note from my editor: *Awwwww!*]

We spent the morning just enjoying ourselves as only newlyweds do.

At about noon, our doorbell rang. We honestly felt like truant school kids who had been caught at the arcade, naked. I'm not sure why we'd be at the arcade naked, but we were naked in our apartment, playing games, so it was kind of like an arcade.

After making himself presentable, Brian answered the door. It was our neighbor. The cop. It's always good to have a cop as a neighbor—until he comes knocking on your door in the middle of the day. That couldn't be good, right?

"Are you OK?" The cop asked Brian. Really? Did our schools send a *cop* to check out whether or not we were really sick? Weren't there drug dealers on some street corner he could bust? Wasn't there a jaywalker wrecking havoc on the lunchtime traffic that he could harass?

Brian stammered our excuses, "Well, uh … my wife has laryngitis and she can't talk. Feels just fine, but can't talk and that won't work too well in a middle school classroom. And ummm … me? Well, I, uhhhhh, ummmmm, I have a headache. Well, I had a headache and um … my stomach. It's kind of hurting. And uhhh … I have a low-grade ear ache and ummm … my pinky toe has been cramping. I feel much better than I did, but still, ummm … not good. Ya know?"

"Sure," the cop said with just a hint of skepticism, or maybe jealousy (I had met his wife and she did not seem to be the kind to lose her voice on Valentine's Day for her man) in his voice, "But, your truck's been running since I left the parking lot at six this morning."

Apparently, Brian had warmed up his truck for his cold-winter's drive to work but forgot to go turn it off when he fell ill.

That half-tank of gas that Brian wasted for me our first Valentine's Day was worth all the roses and chocolate in the world.

Well, maybe not the chocolate part.

I Have No Soccer Magnet

Before we had kids, Brian and I had all the answers to child rearing (remember my heart-felt introduction?). Complete and total experts were we!

We even had an idea of exactly what activities our kids would participate in. Dance? Yes in small doses and only if I could be the backstage mom so as to actually monitor exactly how many fake lashes we attached.

Cheerleading? Hell no—not even if we live in south Texas.

Softball? Yes. Golf? Absolutely! Basketball? You bet!

Fashion Modeling? Only if it pays really, really well and only if we don't go all Jon Benet.

Girl Scouts? Only before cookie season. 'Cause I can name one momma who did not want to lug fifty boxes of mint cookies all over the neighborhood for a $5 credit towards a $250 week-long day camp that I wasn't even invited to. (It's me. I am that momma.)

Soccer—the quintessential sport of little kids worldwide??? No. Way. Wait—that's not right: Soccer? No way in HELL! Seriously, slap a coat of whitewash on a fence and watch it dry. THAT, my friends, is more exciting to me than soccer.

It's not that we totally dismissed soccer all together. We had tried to like soccer. We had tried to understand soccer. We had tried to jump on board the soccer train. Really, we did. We'd catch a soccer match or game or whatever it's called on TV and really try to make sense of it. And by the time the game ended, the score was nuthin' to one, and we were out of breath. Okay, fine. We were out of breath because we'd get bored watching soccer, and Brian would have scored a goal on the couch, if you know what I mean—wink, wink, nudge, nudge!! But still …

The game of soccer made no sense to me or my man, whatsoever. That's really saying something considering Brian is a self-proclaimed athletic junkie. I, on the other hand, have no concept of athletic notions at all, but am a self-proclaimed athletic supporter.

Oh hush. You know what I mean.

Betwixt the two of us, soccer really had us mystified. So when we'd drive by the soccer fields planted firmly in the middle of town (on all three major thoroughfares in our town), we'd laugh at the pitiful parents who had to lug their soccer chairs and their ice chests from their soccer-mom-magnet-emblazed SUVs and sit for an hour watching their little precious run approximately forty-two miles and score only one goal. AND? The parents wouldn't get to have sex in the middle of the game. Just goes to show how smart we were before kids.

I wish now we had laughed at the millionaires who had to spend their weekends in Tahiti because they had nothing better to do.

I have only myself to blame. When our first-born daughter, was old enough to register for soccer, by golly I signed her up and signed her up quick. She was 4 and could read and had stopped taking naps three years earlier; I would have signed her up for liverwurst making if it would have given me a break for a couple of hours!

Her first team was coached by the Biblical incarnate of Job, otherwise known as the saintly and patient Coach Louis. I loved this man. He took Daughter 1 for an hour a week to practice. Thankfully, we met at a local playground, which thus provided Daughter 2 momma-less entertainment while Daughter 1 learned the finer skills of shirt removal—just like Brandi Chastain who ceremoniously removed her jersey in response to her team's win. But Daughter 1 removed her shirt just because she could.

Coach Louis had more patience than Mister Rogers himself after he put on the sweater! Our team started with four girls and six boys. By game three there were six boys and one girl, my precious Daughter 1. By game four there were five boys and one girl. By practice five, all the players wanted to play skins. I was just so happy to have any kind of break from the high-maintenance parenting I was having to do with Daughter 1 that I didn't care one bit that she played topless—whatever pays for college; can I get an "Amen"?

In this league, we played two simultaneous half-field games of three-on-three, a total of eight, five-minute periods. Confused? Yeah, me too.

This meant that our team of six played the entire game with no breaks, except for the occasional trip to the port-a-potty and the full-stop pauses that happened when the often-screaming fire trucks passed right by our fields, which caused all the little players to stop where they were and stare at the highway with their little mouths agape. Because Brian loves to be involved and is a former coach, he kept the time (don't tell him, but it's the grown-up version of water boy). Toward the end of the season, when important football games like Oklahoma vs. Oklahoma State were played in the afternoons, our playing periods lasted a paltry three and a half minutes.

At half time, the moms would supply a healthy snack of water and fruit. After the game, the sugars and complex carbs made their appearance. This was one part of the game I really didn't look forward to: being a soccer mom. I had no patience for the moms who stayed up all night icing soccer patterns into sugar cookies or carving apples into little goals. My idea of soccer snacks was Little Debbie's Zebra cakes—they were the same color as soccer balls. Close enough, right?

One overachieving mom took on the role of team mom (read: General McArthur) and coordinated snacks and the end of year party. I was totally fine to lug my lawn chair (NOT with the matching team color) out of my minivan (without a soccer magnet) and watch my daughter play for one hour a week and bring snacks every sixth week of a twelve-week season. That was until week four. When we played The Bright Yellow Team.

The Bright Yellow Team came out of their Bright Yellow smoke-filled tunnel and assembled on their Bright Yellow bench. The half-time water bottles had little yellow label wraps, personalized with a message for each kid, by name. I wasn't even sure a couple of our boys had names.

They had a helium tank that they used to fill up Bright Yellow balloons at the end of the game that spelled out SPRIT. One of the "I" balloons popped. I didn't know their team name, but for the first time in my life, I wanted to be a soccer mom if for no other reason than to put that obnoxious team to shame. See, while I'm not an athletic-type, I am extremely competitive. And this particular game was The Game where I proudly used my Momma-in-the-stands voice for the very first time. I had succumbed to Soccer-Mom-dom. (Soccer-Mom-dumb?)

What you have to understand about Daughter 1, before you hear this part of my story is this: She was a big girl. Literally big, not just that she uses the potty by herself and even, on occasion, wipes. She's a hoss, a Clydesdale of a child; big, yet elegant and graceful. Just being around her makes you want to chug a cold one. When she was born, the kid ranked off the charts in height and weight. She's always been off the charts—by about two years, it seems. She never wore newborn diapers or clothes. She wore a 3T outfit for her first year pictures. When she was four years old and started soccer, she wore a size 7/8 shorts and a size 12 shoe. She's big. She was a head taller than the tallest boy on The Bright Yellow Team who was a head taller than anyone else on his team. I think he was recruited from Russia.

On this particular Saturday, I learned The Bright Yellow Team was good. No, they were *really* good. I know nothing about soccer, but I could tell that this team was well schooled in the finer points of soccer—who even knew those existed? By league regulations, we could only practice one hour a week. I'm certain, however, that the Bright Yellow Team practiced out of the county at night to get in extra practices; and I'm guessing the cute wraps around the water bottles were to hide the Creatine label.

Our team was six-strong and our coach, God love him, was intent on teaching the kids to enjoy the game NOT kick serious Bright Yellow Team butt. So, as my baby girl lumbered behind the leading scorer for The Bright Yellow Team, I hollered, "Stop him!"

Please understand that never before in Daughter 1's entire life has she ever done anything I have told her to do the first time I have told her to do it. Never before has she ever done anything the second or third time I have told her to do it. She's a strong-willed child (read: stubborn) and has a free spirit (read: really stubborn). But on that day, playing The Bright Yellow Team, when I yelled "Stop him!" The girl did it. Correction: MY girl did it! She dove, full body, into his hips, and took the boy down, I tell ya! I slunk down and glanced at Brian (who was letting the quarter go into the fifth minute) he glanced at me and we both grinned sly little grins.

Maybe soccer wasn't so bad after all.

Actual Soccer-Mom Conversation*

SCENE: from the soccer fields at 8:00am on a Saturday
Characters:

Overzealous Mom: wearing an orange shirt emblazoned with a cartoon Cheetah on the front and "#12's Proud Mom" embroidered on the back. She also has a twelve-inch button with Matty's picture on it and soccer-ball ribbons flowing from the button across her chest. She also has soccer ball earrings, a soccer ball bracelet and possibly even a soccer-ball grill in her mouth. I can't remember for sure as I didn't even look directly at her for fear of being drawn into her bizarre alternate soccer-mom universe.

Me: wearing a grey hoodie to cover my chili-stained bar and grill T-shirt and a Pigg Heating and Air hat to hide my unwashed hair. It was too damn early for a shower. Also, Pigg Heating and Air is so a real place. Look it up. Coleman, OK. Tell them I sent ya. Two more referrals and I get a free air filter change.

Overzealous Mom: I'm so thrilled. Today is my day to bring snacks and I was up all night decorating the cookies.

Me: [faking a snore hoping she'll chat with another awake momma]

Overzealous Mom: I even had to drive an hour to the Fine Foods grocery down south to get coconut flavored food coloring. Coconut is Matty's favorite fruit.

Me: It's a fruit?

Overzealous Mom: Oh, yes! We eat fresh coconut at least once a week. We have it flown in from Key West. We came across this darling little coconut grove while we vacationed there three years ago when Matty was just a year old.

Me: We vacationed down to the Motel 6 last summer because they had an indoor pool.

Overzealous Mom: [Oblivious to my actual words] In fact, for their half-time power-booster snack, I chunked up some coconut and paired it with some cheese in these cute little soccer-ball cups I covered in scrapbooking paper.

Me: Do you take Ritalin?

Overzealous Mom: [Still oblivious] I just feel that we really need to make the most of every little moment while the children are little. They grow up so fast and I just want Matty to remember that his mother was the one who served coconut with Gouda. Can you imagine the memories of that child whose mother brought Cheez-Its and M & M's for their power-booster last week?

Me: That poor child. I'll bet her mom looks a lot like me. Wait. I'll bet it was me. But, honestly, I don't remember. Who can remember from one day to the next what cheese is growing in your fridge?

Overzealous Mom: [Silence. I think she's noticed me. She picks up her chair and moves to the other end of the field]

Me: Hey! Where are you going? C'mon back! I wanna try some of that coconut! Never mind—I'll just steal it from Daughter 1 … she won't eat that crap!

* *"Actual", in this particular case, means it could have happened if I had taken the time to speak to the other mothers during the game.*

The Start Of My Hall-Of-Fame Coaching Career

After a few seasons, we could honestly say that we did give soccer a fair shot. We played with Daughter 1 and Daughter 2 until we could take it no longer. In fact, during one rainy game, I snapped a picture. Immediately, everyone at the game raised their faces to the sky looking for lightning. The officials called time-out; waiting for the thunder that always follows lightning. Brian, always a quick thinker, leaned to me and asked in a very hushed whisper, "Is your flash on?" Indeed-the flash was on. While it was our mistake, we are no dummies. (Notice how I included Brian in that little collaboration?)

Instead of admitting our error of artificial lighting, we stood up and proclaimed that this weather was much too unpredictable to play in and others followed. We single-handedly called a soccer game all by ourselves. Try it the next time you're stuck at the fields on a Saturday when there's a chili cook-off down the road at the United Methodist church. Note: This tactic does NOT work when the sun is out … you'll find yourself the only one looking into the scorching, blinding solar-ball of fire. Just trust me. I know.

Normally, The Daughters played soccer in the fall and softball in the spring. For a variety of reasons, mainly because we both had experience in softball in some form or another, this was our preferred sport. We also liked that the league we played in only scheduled games on weeknights and left the weekends free.

Eventually, we were able to bribe The Daughters with fancy pink-colored equipment to play fall softball and give up soccer all together. So, for the price of a pink bat, a purple bat and two fancy-schmancy hitting helmets, Brian and I got our Saturdays back.

Plus, we talked the commissioner into letting the daughters play on the same team—SCORE! ONE SCHEDULE! It helped that we were lucky enough to be friends with the commissioner who was also the daughters' coach. Before practices began, The Commish called and asked if Brian or I could be her assistant coach. I told her that Brian would love that job. He has coached softball, basketball, track and golf—he's a natural for the job.

Then (there's always a then) she asked if I could be Dugout Coach. Wait: Brian gets to hang out by first base and only deal with one kid at a time? And I get offered the job of corralling the cats in the dugout? Ummmm … since The Commish is a good friend of mine and is one of the sweetest, kindest, nicest people I have ever known in my whole entire life, I really hated to tell her no. But I did anyway. No way. No how. Not me.

She threatened to put my girls on two different traveling teams that played on the weekends, and I said I would be pleased as punch to assist her as Dugout Coach. Really: How hard would it be to coach eleven girls in the chant, "Here we go, TEEEAAAAMMM, Here we go [Clap, Clap]"?

Very. That's how hard is was: Very hard.

We played our first game on a beautiful evening in September, and I had my coaching debut. We were visitors, so we were up to bat first. All I had to do was get the right girl to the plate at the appropriate time and get the next girl on deck warming up. Easy! But then, the girl on deck had to go to the bathroom and someone three fields over brought the cutest Chihuahua-weenie dog mix to the ball fields. "Can we go see the Chi-weenie, please?" Before I can tell the little whiners no way, half the team took off. I looked in the dugout and I saw three girls in there. One was texting; one was playing her DS and one, who happens to look a lot like the first base coach and my very own bedmate, was swinging from the center beam. No. I am not kidding.

Finally, we got our three outs and I could take a breather. Oh. Wait. I had to get thirty pounds of catching gear on a thirty-two-pound second grader. I got her geared up and then I *really* got to coach.

"You know what to do, right?" I asked. She shook her heavy head no; "Throw the ball back after it's pitched to you." Great words of wisdom that I don't think Tommy LaSorda could have said any better himself. Or maybe Vince Lombardi couldn't have said them better. Whoever. But, what the hell do I know? What sport is this again?

After the first two pitches flew right past my ducking and screaming catcher, I went back and told her that, as the position's name would indicate, she would have to actually *catch* the ball. Five minutes of tears and a quick equipment change later, we had a new catcher.

This future-World-Series-super star was, indeed, a catcher and caught every ball. Then she threw every pitch to the third baseman. Oh well, this was a learning league, and we needed more fielding practice. Glad I could help.

We headed back into the dugout for our at-bat again, and I positioned myself in the doorway so as to not lose any Chi-weenie enchanted girls. I got my first batter to the plate and my second batter on deck when I heard a train wreck … OR the sound of six bats crashing to the floor. Then the sound of whimpering commences, and I heard one weak apology, “I thought I could juggle the bats. Really.” I would have sent that player right out to her mother except that her mother was standing in the doorway of the dug out wondering why she thought Dug Out Coach would be an easy job. We finished our time at bat and were now back on the field.

I looked on the lineup and saw that we have a different catcher. Oh. Heavens. Really? Do the kids need to know about ALL positions? Couldn’t we just railroad them into one position at the age of 7 and call it good? More equipment changes. This inning, I added more words of wisdom to my coaching repertoire: “After the hitter hits, toss the bat out of the way and cover home.” Again, those words are gonna land me a spot in little league hall of fame, I can feel it.

The first batter hit a screamer right back at the pitcher and dropped her bat. This was what the catcher had been waiting for. She picked up the bat and threw it down the first base line narrowly missing the runner and then dropped to the ground, spread-eagle over home plate. Man! If I didn’t have power over these kids, I didn’t know who would.

Another inning came to an end. And another and another. After four innings, we scored twenty runs and the other team scored eighteen. You don't score like that in the major leagues, people. Or even soccer, as far as that goes. We also had three blisters from poorly positioned catching equipment, a sprained ankle from dropping off the center beam of the dugout, two goose eggs from a juggling show and one Chi-weenie puppy. I don't know how many of you are familiar with coaching, but I tell you what: none of those things were in my coaching handbook. Wait. I didn't get a handbook. I feel like I have—obviously—gone above and beyond with my coaching abilities.

I also feel that after one game, my very good friend, The Commish, has learned her lesson. I doubt I'll be asked to assist with one of her teams again. I tried to call her and ask how I did and strategize for the next season (that's coach talk, in case you were wondering). But her number's been changed … and there's a "FOR SALE" sign in her front yard. I have heard she moved to Arkansas.

Let Me Tell You About The Flu Bug

Welcome to the house of strep and puke. Here we are at that time of year, again, my friends. The time of year when sick children crawl into bed with Brian and me and keep me awake all night.

Yes, I said *me*. A herd of bison could crawl into bed with my lover and me complaining of stuffy noses, coughs, fevers and headaches while puking on the comforter. Brian would sleep right through it. Or at least pretend to.

In fact, we had several earthquakes in Oklahoma and Brian, though he was in the state, right beside me for every single one of them, has yet to actually experience an earthquake.

Because I work in school with our daughters, we all bring home the same germs. The germ last month was the puking germ. When the puking germ hits our house, I'm sorta grateful for ceramic tile. The good thing about tile is that it's easy to clean up. The bad thing about tile is that is splatters. All. Over. It's typically not something I save for the housekeeper to clean up either, so I have to clean it up myself. Also, I don't actually have a housekeeper.

Daughter 1 started us off with a rousing round of regurgitation on Monday morning. At 12:32am, to be exact. Why is it that kids never get sick when I'm wide awake and functioning and able to string together words from the English language in a coherent thought?

Daughter 2, my baby, continued the tradition the next night or morning … at 2:45. This did wake up Brian, as she didn't even make it out of our bed (she claims our marital bed as her family bed when she's not feeling well) before the projectile puke hit the Percale, as it were. However, he was up, the sheets were changed, and he was back to snoring before Daughter 2 and I even had a chance to decide what clean nighties we'd put on next. Then we assumed the position in the Sick Chair.

I'm not sure when the tradition began, but when either daughter is sick in the middle of the night, Momma and Daughter retreat to the Sick Chair. The Sick Chair is the same thing as Brian's recliner. Only he doesn't use it at night (if he's been a good boy), so we do. And by assuming the position, that means I have got one arm around the sick kid and one hand channel surfing for something that's not an infomercial selling the exact mop we'd need to clean up the splatter on the walls in the bathroom.

We usually watch TV Land. It's during these tender moments of nursing The Daughters back to health that I have led them to know such classics as *The Brady Bunch* and *The Addams Family* and *Cheers*. OK—when *Cheers* came on, I thought Daughter 1 was asleep. A few hours later explaining the dangers and toils of sleeping around while single taught me to be more thorough in my sleep checking. "But, Momma, doesn't he love her? Why aren't they married?"

This is the sight you'll see when one of our daughters is sick: I am plopped in the Sick Chair; sick girl in my lap; two, maybe three blankets on top. Sweet, sick child will have a washrag in her mouth and one on her forehead. I will hold, with one hand, a hospital tub ready to catch anything spewing from the sickly child's head. The chair will be reclined just enough to still see the TV but settled in a relaxed position. Eventually, when pitiful baby girl falls asleep, I will try in vain until daybreak to wake up my sweaty arm so I can carry sleeping, sickly beauty to bed. I will never succeed.

In the morning, Brian will think he's sneaking past us on the way to the gym (but you can never truly sneak past a tired, dozing momma who's holding a sick baby) and then return home an hour later to carry his offspring into her own bed. I will stumble drunkenly back toward the bathroom or bed—whichever I can find first—incoherently mumbling about a do-it-yourself vasectomy kit. Brian will sincerely offer to stay home from school to stay with the sick kid or kids. I will insincerely thank him while sharpening and sterilizing scissors according to the internet-snip-snip instructions, but I will tell him that I earned the sick day since I comforted said-sick child through three hours of Steve Urkel before she fell back asleep!

The good thing about my girls is that they never act sick. The bad thing about my girls is that they never act sick. When I take them into the pediatrician's office, other children are acting sick. Other children cling to their Mommas; some children whine; others hold their heads between their hands and shiver. My Daughters run around chasing the fish in the fish tank and draw pictures on the walls and yell out, "My turn yet?" every time a nurse opens the door to call a truly sick child back.

When we finally are escorted to the examination room, and the sick child is jumping up on the exam table or picking out her favorite make-a-noise book from the book basket or drinking out of the way-cool-our-Momma-never-buys-us-SpongeBob-cups, the nurse always asks me, "What are we seeing your, uh, 'sick child' for today?" Yes, I can actually hear the quotes around 'sick child' in the tone of her voice.

It doesn't matter what I say, I'm pretty sure the notes she's making in the chart read: *Neurotic mom – nothing wrong with annoying kid.*

Thank heavens our pediatrician is kind and loves my girls. She takes her time and always confirms that they are, indeed, sick.

Upon receiving that confirmation, I push the not-so-sick-acting kid off the examining table and begin to snooze. It was me, after all, who was up all night cleaning splattered walls, watching *Beverly Hillbillies* and wildly spraying Lysol with my half-asleep hand after each little sniffle.

I'm just glad they did not charge me a co-pay when I finally woke up.

Things Overhead in the Waiting Room of the Pediatrician's Office

(Strangely enough, these words comfort me)

From another momma after snapping her flip phone shut: "Ronald? Did you unplug the refrigerator at home?"

Random child with green snot dripping from her nose sitting way too close to my child: "Then my momma opened the box to dinner and popped it in the microwave."

Random child sitting beside me seemingly belonging to no one: "Do you wear pajamas? Because my momma and daddy don't always wear pajamas at night in bed."

Random child with ripped shirt and dirty fingernails: "We used to have a dog and I tied him to the swing set so he could swing with me, but then when the gate was left open when I dragged the spare tire to the back yard, he got out and I haven't seen him since."

Random child with no shoes on: "Sometimes when my momma is up late at night and too tired, she gets silly and wears only an apron and dusts my dad with a feather duster."

Random child hand-fishing in the aquarium: "I don't know why my momma was so mad—all I did was pee in her bed."

Random child emerging from the bathroom, probably after NOT washing his hands: "My brother and I are having a contest in our bathroom to see how long we can go without flushing the toilet."

From another momma who is holding her cellphone to her chest: "Tabitha? Daddy wants to know if you dumped the dish soap in the washing machine."

Random child sitting crisscross-applesauce right in front of me: "I'm not wearing any underwear today because my momma said to put on my pants and shirt, but she didn't say underwear."

Random child playing with the free lotion samples: "My momma always cleans the kitchen before she goes to bed, but in the morning, there are always two big, long glasses in the sink."

Random momma talking way too loud on the phone: "I hope to GAWD they clear him to go back to school this afternoon. I have already taken a couple of days off work, and I could really use the break."

Not Much Has Changed Since I Was Eight

As a grown up, I don't mind going to the doctor nearly as much as I did as a child. When I was a child, it seemed that every stinkin' time I went to the doctor, I ended up with a shot right in my butt. After a few visits with my pediatrician, he became wise and started using the grown-up word when in my presence: *Injection*. And after a few times of hearing that word, I became wise and my vocabulary was expanded. No Child Left Behind has nothing on a doctor who's avoiding a kid who's a runner.

Eventually, as we all do, I grew up. Not in that I learned to take my shots and be done with it; rather, in that I started going to grown up doctors who didn't always give grown ups shots. And truth be told, knowing that I would have to get shots (or have blood drawn or be poked in any way, shape or form) really was the best birth control for this shot-a-phobic high school junior!

Every year since I have been teaching, I have gotten strep throat at least once. I teach. I know that desperate mommas everywhere will Motrin-up a kid and send him or her to school in the morning on that off chance that their 104 degree fever and burning throat is "nothing big." Hell! I'm that momma on occasions, too. But by the time the Motrin wears off and the kid has passed out in her own puke, everyone in the classroom is infested with the germs. Including the teacher, which is me. We teachers are so exposed to many varied germs on any given day, that we say, "BRING ON THE SUPER VIRUS! We ain't afraid of no bug!"

But, on occasion, we're so worn down and our bodies' own defenses are worn down that we succumb to any of the massive amounts of germs that reside in America's classrooms. My nemesis germ is strep. So, last week, when I began feeling achy, and my throat began to feel burn-y, and my head began to pound, and my body began to chill, I knew I had been got. I had a new doctor, whom I dearly loved as she really did seem to care for me. Added bonus: She was a harried momma as well, so she related to me. My plan was to call her up, get my antibiotics and in just a few days, I'd be halfway back to normal. I never was fully normal anyway.

I waited for her in the examination room, shivering and moaning. She came in, did a quick assessment and pronounced that since she had seen no less than twenty-six dozen cases of strep since eight that morning, that's what I had.

"But, don't fret!" she assured me. She'd have me fixed up in no time at all. The nurse would be in shortly to give me an injection.

"Say wha-???" I murmured from my almost-comatose state.

"An injection. A shot. I know you're a very busy momma and you don't have the time to mess with ten days of pills. With this injection, you'll be good as new in the morning!"

"You know?" I argued, trying to muster up the strength to pick up my purse and get the hell outta Dodge, "I don't mind ten days of pills. It'll keep me out of trouble if I have to keep track of ten days of pills. Plus, I don't really need to be good as new by morning. I'm not *that* busy! My family will do just fine without me for a week or so."

"Oh, Heather!" she laughed, "Don't be ridiculous. A little shot is nothing." And with that little giggle she left. She shut the door behind her and I had flashbacks to my pediatrician locking me in my room as a 6 year old who had an escape plan.

She knew—she absolutely *knew*—that I didn't have the strength to turn the knob and pull open the door. I was trapped. So, I just rolled over on the examining table and wept. Who, for heaven's sakes, gets a SHOT when she's 40??!?! Had my doctor mistaken me for a child? Heck, even The Daughter's pediatrician doesn't give them injections unless the school requires it. And they have extra staff on hand to help hold The Daughters down. Oh. My. Gawd. I briefly wondered how many nurses it would take to hold me down on this very day.

I decided that I wouldn't be a crybaby. I would suck it up and take my shot and just pretend to be sick for more days, because hey! If I'm feeling this bad right now, I want to milk it for all it's worth with my family. So, I unbuttoned my shirt and pulled my left arm out of the sleeve, letting the rest of the shirt drape halfway across my body. Then I waited and sweated and fretted until the nurse finally arrived with the needle.

"OK, Hon," she said in her best pediatric voice; she must have heard me whimpering. "Let's get you turned over and we'll get you all fixed up."

Turned over? My other arm? OK … so I took my right arm out of my shirt, now my half buttoned blouse was draped across my waist. C'mon, now—let's just get this over with.

"Oh, no, honey," the nurse consoled. "The shot is going in your hiney." Now, I knew she was messing with me.

"Hiney?" I chuckled as drool escaped from my mouth.

"Oh yes. I'll just need you to turn around and drop your drawers." She said sounding way too chipper for a woman I was about to kick in the gut.

I needed a plan. I know! I would just pretend I didn't hear that part. I wiped my chin and then I held out my left arm to her. She gently put her hand on my arm, looked at me, then said in a voice that is normally reserved for the very old and hard of hearing or those who speak a different language, "I WILL HAVE TO GIVE YOU THE SHOT IN YOUR BUTTOCKS. PLEASE BEND OVER."

Sigh. I was cornered. I couldn't very well sprint from the office now. Even if I felt like it, my shirt was down around my waist. I had no choice but to comply. I stood up; I unfastened my pants; I dropped my pants to my knees; I lowered my white cotton granny panties to just below my bum and leaned over on the table. I was nervous. I was feeling like poo-poo. I was hyperventilating just thinking about the incoming needle.

And then it happened: The not-so-small little pinch on my hiney.

And then …

And then …

And then I felt it: The wet cloth on my head and the multiple hands putting me back up on the table.

And then I heard it: My doctor's voice saying, "So she just passed out?"

And then the nurse confirmed it: “She was leaning on the table and then she just flopped right over!”

And then I remembered: I was, for all intents and purposes, half-naked.

In the same voice the nurse had used with me just moments before my face met the tile, she spoke again, “YOU PASSED OUT, MRS. DAVIS. ARE YOU ALRIGHT?” In response, I just shut my eyes. There’s no need to state the obvious when your butt is exposed and your shirt is bunched up at your waist.

I don’t remember how I got home, but I did get there and don’t remember a thing until about six the next morning when I had to pee.

The doctor was right. In the morning, I felt much better than I had. I mean, my elbows and knees were feeling a little bit sore from the impact, but, otherwise, my doctor actually knew what she was talking about—too bad I can never go back to her office again.

No, no, no … it’s not that I’m embarrassed. They are medical professionals. They’ve seen naked bodies much worse than mine! It’s totally that she gives shots. And that can never, ever, *never* happen to me again.

One Giant Step For Tweens, One Tiny Step Toward Womanhood

Daughter 1 is pretty picky about her clothing. Her undies have to match with the waistband. What if an outfit doesn't have a waistband? It is not going on her body. The sleeves have to be form fitting and can't go below her elbow or on top of her shoulder. One day, I just know I'll be really thankful that she's that particular about clothing. Until then, I'll start each morning with some vodka in my OJ just to get me through her dressing routine, which usually runs about ten minutes after we need to leave the house.

As OCD as Daughter 1 is about her clothing, it was not with great joy or certain regret or even a touch of nostalgia that I took her to buy her first bra. In fact, the feeling in my heart—no, not my heart—deep in my gut was a wrenching feeling of think-I'm-gonna-puke in combination with Can-I-get-a-mother-and-daughter-prescription-for-some-Xanax? I don't recall much about when my mom and I bought my first bra (other than she folded the bra in half and made me try it on over my shirt and shoulders right there in the "Growing Girls" section of the TG & Y. Not that I harbor any ill feelings. Anymore. (Note from my Editor: *What is this TG & Y you speak of? Is it a place?*) (Note from me to my Editor: *TG & Y was a Hellmart-type place before Hellmart took over the world.*)

Daughter 1 has always been a big girl. When she was born, she was the third girl born on that day within an hour. The other babies were 6 lbs. 2 oz. and 6 lbs. 4 oz. Daughter 1 was 9 lbs. 6 oz. and 22 ½ inches long. She didn't even fit into newborn diapers. And she looked like she could eat the other babies. I think the other parents were a bit fearful. Since she was my child and I was going to be the one nursing her, I was a bit fearful as well.

Even now, she stands head and shoulders above her peers. So, it's not a complete surprise that she, as she prepared to enter fourth grade, had to get a bra.

I had known she would need this kind of support pretty soon, but I also know Daughter 1. This is the child that will change pants four times in the morning if the inseam of her jeans twists just a little bit to the front or the back and doesn't stay on the invisible inseam line. One time, Brian had to take her home from Sunday school because her zipper felt "wonky" and she wouldn't quit fidgeting with it. Truth be told, the fidgeting was irritating Brian and he couldn't stand it one minute more, plus he didn't mind missing church that day.

I could only imagine how this child will fare with an over-the-shoulder boulder holder. Not that she had boulders. Yet.

I knew it was time to get her a brassiere when Brian-unobservant as he is-texted me as we sat across the table from each other at a family reunion, saying, "H need brz."

I texted back the international symbol for "what": *???*

And he texted back: BRA.

That, my friends, is how Brian and I conversed about this monumental occasion in Daughter 1's life.

I brought up the idea of a bra several times to Daughter 1 to get her used to the idea. She brought up the terms *push up*, *padded*, *underwire* and *front hook*. Say who?

I believe I'll take this moment to thank the *iCarly* cast and crew for allowing my daughter to expand her undergarment vocabulary. We were further along in the process than we thought! I measured her and discovered that the words *push up*, *padded*, *underwire* and *front hook* were not that far off.

She and I made a special day of it, going to Hellmart to pick out her first bra. I remembered my first bra. It was plain, and it was white. It was plain and white because that was my one and only choice. Oh! I did have the choice between a small pink flower front and center or no flower. I chose the flower and promptly pulled it off playing with my bra the next day.

Daughter 1 and I gallantly and humbly made our way to the baby bra aisle, there were no plain bras, and there were no white bras. This girl had more selection than I did over in the saggy momma section. I seriously looked to see if there was a bra that would fit me in this department because they were all colorful and cute.

For try-on purposes, we selected an orange and green striped knit bra … much to the dismay of Daughter 1 who wanted to try on a turquoise and pink padded underwire bra that had "Love Me Now" scrawled in graffiti all over the cups. If ever I want to cash in on Brian's life insurance policy via his having a cardiac arrest, I just might let Daughter 1 bring home this particular bra.

We went off to the dressing room, where Daughter 1 proceeded to attempt to hook her bra for the first time.

And attempted again. Then attempted again. And yet again. And again. I forgot the total stress and anguish hooking and unhooking a bra could inflict! Finally, with the experienced fingers that only a 40-year old momma can have, the bra was hooked, adjusted and ready for inspection. She pranced. Then she danced. Then she twisted. Then she pretended to be sitting in her fourth grade classroom and raising her hand to answer the question that every fourth grade teacher asks on the first day of school, "Who is wearing a bra today?"

Finally, we decided we had the appropriate size and then we began the actual selection process. The "Love Me Now" bra was completely off the table … I did waver some when she offered to do her "own laundry for the rest of my life!" but ultimately decided that I would not pay for that kind of slut-in-training bra. Period. (Maybe I am that kind of mother.) Plus, I totally didn't believe she would do any laundry until the day *I* died.

In prepping her for bra wearing, I told her she'd have to change bras at least every other day. I figured this would be a deal breaker for Miss Blue-And-Brown-Striped-Sweater-four-times-a-week. Instead, she did the math and figured that she'd need at least four bras. At least.

Since the style she really loved the best (except for the "Love Me Now" tramp-maker) came in packages of three, she ended up with six bras. That's approximately five and a half more than I currently have in my dresser. Daughter 1 is now the proud owner of a blue bra, a green bra, a pink bra, a white polka-dot bra, a grey bra and a rainbow striped bra.

Immediately she came home and decided to wear the green bra. She went to her room and spent ten minutes there with the door closed. When she came out, she sat right down as if nothing were different.

"Well?" I questioned, "How's it feel?"

"Just fine," Daughter 1 answered back.

"Just fine? You're feeling comfortable?" I asked waiting for the clothing obsession to set in and the fidgeting to begin.

"Well," she said slowly, "Since I couldn't get it fastened, I'll start wearing bras tomorrow."

That's right, Scarlett, think about that tomorrow.

Underwear? Under Where?

My mother's favorite subject when I'm dressed up? Undergarments. What? You aren't familiar with that archaic term? Let me help ya out here: Bras, panties, undies, lingerie, camisoles, slips, girdles, G-strings … and all that other stuff. It very well could be my mother's favorite topic of conversation with me. When she's not talking about chin hair, of course.

The conversation starts in much the same way every single time I'm dressed up: I will no sooner wear a dress to a funeral, wedding, church or other rare-dress-wearing occasions and my mom will say this: Are you wearing a slip? It's as predictable as the fact that tomorrow the day will end in Y. Now, she knows that I don't even own a slip. I haven't worn a slip since I graduated from high school. She thinks I wore one on my wedding day, but it was actually a nightie. Shhhh … Don't tell her.

I repeat to her for the 36,362th time since becoming an adult that I don't own a slip I'm not even certain can you even buy a slip any more outside of estate sales. (Note from my Editor: *Yes you can buy slips outside of estate sales. I'm a proponent for slips, especially in Oklahoma wind.*) (Note from me to my Editor: *Did my mom pay you to say that?*)

My own momma will say, "Well you should have worn a girdle at least." A girdle? Really? I thought those were outlawed with the nineteenth amendment which states, and I quote: *The right of citizens of the United States to vote shall not be denied or abridged by the*

United States or by any State on account of sex and furthermore women shall never, ever, never wear girdles. In answer to my mom's question, I squish my eyebrows together and glare at her from the corners of my eyes just like I did at age 6 when she said I had to at least *try* the Brussels sprout. And really, in terms of torture devices, girdles and Brussels sprouts are in the very same family. (Note from my Editor: *I made Brussels sprouts sautéed in bacon tonight. They were AMAZEBALLS*!) (Note from me to my Editor: *Why are you on my mom's side?*)

Then my mom brings up pantyhose. "Thank heavens for control top, right?" I know at this point that she's not even paying attention to anything I'm wearing. If she were, she'd know that I'm not wearing pantyhose because a) they haven't made pantyhose in 'pasty white' since 1989 and b) panty hose don't have stubble.

Daughter 2 and I recently accompanied my mom to the wedding of one of her oldest and dearest friends. Her friend, at the age of 80, was being married after over forty years of being single. She had met her betrothed at the assisted nursing facility where they were marrying on this particular Saturday night. When she got into the minivan, my mom looked over at my slacks and said, "Aren't you wearing a dress to the wedding?"

I looked over at her slacks and said, "Aren't you wearing a dress to the wedding?"

I have to admit: It was one of my better attempts at avoiding the undergarment guilt.

Poor Daughter 2, though, *she* wore a dress. And a cute little linen dress it was. I could see the relief in my mom's face when she noticed that Daughter 2 was in a dress. The undergarment conversation would not die on this hill, no sir.

"Daughter 2, that's a very cute dress," my mom complimented her with a genuine smile. My jaw dropped open at the thought of my mom not bringing up undergarments. Perhaps her time was drawing nigh.

Once we arrived at the ceremony, I hustled my blown-after-two-big-babies-bladder to the restroom and returned to find my mom leaning down speaking almost directly into Daughter 2's ear. Daughter 2's poor face was a perfect blend of confusion and amusement.

As I sat down beside Daughter 2, with my mom on her other side, Daughter 2 leaned over to me and said, "Nana just told me a story about wearing slips under dresses. Are slips like little pieces of paper?" My mom heard her comment and rolled her eyes, probably utterly depressed that I was failing so miserably as a momma.

I sighed and explained to Daughter 2 that a slip was an article of clothing that women (maybe some men) wore under their dresses to keep their dresses from being seen through. "But," I comforted my innocent baby girl, "Your dresses all have built-in slips called liners." I said this loud enough for my mom and any other archaic slip-supporter to hear.

"Oh, thank goodness," Daughter 2 said, visibly releasing the stress from her shoulders, "I thought Nana was making up stuff."

And just like that, the topic of undergarments dies with a generation.

This One Time? At Vegas?

Brian just returned from a solo-trip to Vegas. It wasn't totally solo. It was a work thing, but Vegas without the whole fam-damily has got to leave all other times and places looking really, well, boring.

It was a four-day event at The Riviera, home of the Zany Girls All Female Revue or some other such show with a likewise snappy title. It was a legit conference. I checked it out with the hotel, the conference organization and the BBB. Seriously. It sounded boring; I believed he was going to learn. Or work. Or whatever.

Before leaving, Brian asked how I'd feel if he went to the Zany Girls All Female Revue. I told him he was a big boy and was capable of making his own decisions and, whatever he decided, he would totally be able to sleep on the couch when he came home.

Actually, I didn't mind at all him attending the show. What I objected to, with a resounding "Hellz to the No," was his spending $125 to see Zany Girls All Female Revue. Here … give me $125, shine a flashlight on me and I'll go crazy for ya. In fact, since I know and love Brian so well, I'll give him front row tickets to my little show for the low, low rate of $70.

He argued that his being in Vegas and seeing this particular show was a once in a lifetime opportunity. I argued that this would be his second trip to Vegas in his one lifetime, so it's a good thing he doesn't work as an accountant or a math teacher. Oh wait …

Deflated but not resigned, Brian did his research and

came up with an alternative plan: Instead, of Zany Girls All Female Revue for $125, Brian, who is such a dealer, somehow scored free tickets to *Sin Cit-ay All Female Show*. Free? I can do! Go with my blessing. Of course, tickets to my flashlight show just went back up to $125.

I, however, was not in Vegas. I was at home. With two crazy daughters. AND, I'm willing to bet that I got more action in one night than Brian did while at *Sin Cit-ay*. Let me break this down for you.

At 8:30 on Monday night, I sent the daughters to the bathroom to brush their teeth, wash their faces and get ready for bed. Brian headed to the buffet down the strip to eat rib eyes and crab legs for $3 a person.

At 9:00, I turned off the lights for the daughters and kissed them goodnight. Brian got thirds on crab legs.

At 9:30, I got a drink for Daughter 1. Brian also got a drink. For himself.

At 9:45, I argued with Daughter 2 about whether or not she heard a creepy noise. Brian got his picture taken with a creepy showgirl down on Fremont.

At 10:15, I called Brian to tell him goodnight. Brian thought he felt a vibration in his pocket, but it's crowded in the line for the show and he blows it off.

At 11:00, Daughter 2 climbed in bed with me because it *was* a creepy noise, and she didn't care what I thought. Brian climbed into his chair at the show.

At 11:30, Daughter 2 peed my bed. I was up changing the sheets. Daughter 1 woke up wondering what I was doing. I got the sheets changed and found I had two additional people in bed with me. Brian was listening to "the most talented singer" he's ever heard. He chose to share this with me through a text—because a phone call would be distracting during this particular part of the show. But he did want to share the shock and surprise of this extremely talented (and topless, but this supposedly escapes his thoughts) singer with me. To quote his text: "Seriously she's the best singer."

At 12:45, I woke up thinking I heard the doorbell. I laid in bed wondering why our doorbell would be ringing and thinking that maybe Daughter 2 was right. There really were creepy noises in our house. I squeezed my eyes shut and fell back to sleep with Daughter 2's knees in my back and Daughter 1's elbow in my ear. During intermission, Brian discovered that I had called. He texted, "Are you asleep?" and awaited my reply. Opening just one eye, I wondered if our doorbell has always sounded like my text-tone. I got up and put Brian's prized golf driver beside the bed.

At 2:00, I finally got back to sleep after deciding that there's really no creepy noise and the doorbell must have been something else ... like a text. Brian decided that maybe one round of blackjack before heading to bed wouldn't be too bad.

At 3:30, The Daughters, in their sleep, began talking simultaneously and ultimately ended up arguing, in their sleep, with each other about whose turn it is to feed the sheep. We don't have sheep. Brian hits 21 and decides to walk away with an additional $15 in his pocket. Big winner.

At 4:30, I finally got back to sleep and Brian turns in after watching *CSI*. Really. Who watches *CSI: Las Vegas* while *in* Vegas?

At 5:30, my alarm went off and I whimpered. By the time I got into the shower, it was a full-blown sob!

At 9:30, Brian texted me and asked how my night

was. I turned my phone off for the rest of the day.

That, my friends, was the end of day one.

The next time he goes to Vegas, he's taking The Daughters. I'm staying home and resting.

I May Know My Snooze Button A Little Too Intimately

At the end of the summer, I find myself very, very cranky. The main reason I'm cranky is that I have to start the retraining process for school hours. All summer long, we've been swimming in the dark and making midnight runs for ice cream and watching all the best movies that are available on DVR. We've been living the life. But unfortunately, the good life must end and school must begin. We must train ourselves to wake up early once again.

I take this task very seriously because I have to retrain myself as well. As a teacher, I typically spend the last several weeks of my summer vacations going to workshops and trainings and in-services. This year, however, I got lucky. I had all of July to do nothing … and the one thing I had been fortunate enough to do is sleep in.

The good news is that Daughter 2 is just like me in that she wakes up when she has to go to the bathroom, which may be about eleven-ish or so. Daughter 1, on the other hand, is just like Brian. They both have a time to get up and it's earlier than I care to know, unless there's a fire, then please, wake me up. Otherwise, don't talk to me before 9:30 during the summer. Just don't.

Last night, we started our training for school time. The daughters were in bed and asleep by 8:30. Lucky me. I took advantage of the quiet time to get caught up on my DVR shows (which are all reruns anyway—it's the summer, so it's all episodes of *Friends*). After Rachel and Ross got back together but before they broke up again, I read a little, and then I updated my Facebook status, twice. I glanced at my phone: it was after midnight, quickly approaching one, and I decided that I had better go to sleep. Before turning off the light, I set my alarm for 7:30. I figured if I let it snooze for about thirty minutes, then I could ease into my normal wake-up time by the end of the week. Good plan.

My alarm went off, and I hit snooze. No, "hit" is, perhaps, not the right word. I bitch-slapped the snooze button. It went off again and I punched that sonova again. It went off again, and I snoozed again. Finally, I took that noisy contraption into my arms in bed with me. I discovered that if I slept *with* the alarm, I could feel the vibration before I heard the alarm and I could hit snooze before it actually jarred me fully awake.

Daughter 1 came in to tell me that she was making herself a sandwich for breakfast … or a sandcastle from peanuts. I can't remember exactly what she said. I hit snooze again.

Daughter 2 crawled in bed with me and scooted me right off my pillow. I jumped up out of bed and dragged myself to Brian's pillow. I hit snooze again.

Finally, I told myself that enough was enough. I had to get up and get in the school routine and this morning might as well be the first day of that training… then I stretched. Then I hit snooze again.

I finally got up when Daughter 1 told me she was now going to make grilled cheese sandwiches for us all for lunch.

This routine went on and on and on until finally, my principal called and said I had a very important decision to make. He said I could decide to keep hitting snooze, or I could keep my job. Since I have become accustomed to luxuries like electricity and running water, I chose to wake up. But only because he was so persuasive.

Despite my very rigorous "hitting snooze" routine, school did start and we all did have to get up out of bed and go to school. I read my contract and didn't see where it said that I exactly had to be in the classroom, but my principal assures me that language is in there somewhere. So, like it or not, we began our early mornings—again. Damn that man.

I'm not sure if I have mentioned this before or not, but I'm not a morning person. Never have been; never will be. Don't even want to be. As a direct result of my inability to function as any kind of human being before 10:30am, getting ready for school every morning is not a pleasant experience at our house. For me. Probably for everyone else, too, but I'm not awake enough to actually notice. Or care.

The problem lies with Daughter 1. See, Daughter 2 is exactly like me: She will sleep until she absolutely has to get up. So, in the mornings, I set her clothes on her bed and she gets dressed under the covers then runs out the door when I yell that I'm leaving.

Daughter 1? She's very much a morning person. Regardless of what time she goes to bed, she is wide-awake by 6:30. She gets this from Brian, who rises at 5:30 every morning without fail. Sometimes I wish we had eggs to gather or cows to milk so that he would have a reason to get up and not turn on the television.

The Elusive, Exactly Perfect Outfit

The problem with Daughter 1 being up and awake at such an ungodly hour is that I can't just set out clothes for her to put on-she has an issue with 99.9 percent of all outfits I pick out for her.

Seeing this as the dispute, I let her pick out her outfits the night before. In the morning this works out simply: She has an issue with 99.9 percent of all outfits that *she* picks out as well. The jeans don't fit right; the sleeves are too long; the shirt won't go down over her belt; the pants are too low; the pants are too high; the sleeves are too short; the shirt shows her breasts if she pulls it six inches down from her neck. The particular pickiness goes on and on and on.

She gets this utter pickiness from Brian as well. Unfortunately, Brian is usually up and out the door before we even start our morning whining. Routine! I mean routine.

This past week, however, I was out of town and Brian had to get the daughters ready in the morning all by himself. Go ahead: I laughed, too. When I got back into town, Brian proclaimed that something had to be done about Daughter 1's wardrobe.

Hell yes, something has to be done. I was attaining no less than one hundred strands of grey hair every single morning because of that child and her war on clothing. Let's bring in Jimmy Carter for a peace-making effort to get this morning trauma under control.

"It's insane!" he complained the night I arrived back home, "We went through all of her shirts but three before she decided on one that would work!"

After I wiped the tears from my eyes and stopped giggling, I welcomed him to my own personal purgatory, flights arriving every morning beginning at 6:15.

As a result of Daughter 1 pulling clothes out of her closet at will and trying on no less than 47 outfits a morning, her laundry pile equals that of mine, Brian's and Daughter 2's combined. This weekend, when Brian volunteered to help put all the laundry away and noticed that it was all put away except Daughter 1's, he decided that *this* was the time to do something about Daughter 1's clothing issues.

"I'm going to get a handle on this," he announced with some kind of utopian authority that only comes from delusional personalities.

Giggling, I let him and Daughter 1 attack her closet and her drawers with all the passion of the Olympic Curling Team—whom, I'm sure, would have a heyday with my bathroom floor. And I'm willing to let them use any of my floor surfaces for practice. I wouldn't even charge them. Go USA!

I, on the other hand, poured myself a glass of sangria and situated a camp chair in the hall so that I could take in the full show. I even snapped a couple of pictures to put in our scrapbook. These are the makings of memories, my friends.

About three minutes into the "Does this fit? Will you wear it?" show, Daughter 1 emerged naked and said, "He wants to get rid of the red and pink top!" I reminded her that she doesn't like it; she says it shows her chest too much. "But, it's so pretty!" She protested! Brian yelled for her to return to her room, she slumped her shoulders and slinked back and the show continued.

Approximately seven minutes later she stormed out to me wearing a *High School Musical* Shirt. “It’s not too tight, is it?” she asked. I reminded her that it was her little sister’s shirt and she sulked back in.

I actually heard Brian say, “HSM is so yesterday, girlfriend!”

I heard protests of, “It’s cute!”

“It matches one that your BFF has!”

“It’s soft and silky!”

And “All the kids are wearing this!”

Then, I heard Daughter 1 arguing back, “But Daddy you don’t know *anything*!”

Two glasses of the sweetest sangria and five lawn bags full of too small, too short, too big or never gonna wear it clothing later, the fashion duo emerge from her bedroom looking victorious.

Brian smugly announced, “We won’t have one single problem with our outfits from here on out!”

Daughter 1 announced, “I get to wear my sweat suit to school everyday!”

“Everyday?” I question them, glancing between dad and daughter.

“That’s all I have left!” Daughter 1 exclaimed.

Stacy London has nothing on Brian.

Craziest things I have ever heard as I'm lying in bed at some ungodly, early hour pretending my family is not wrecking the house

From Brian: Honey, do you want to buy steaks from this guy on the front porch?

From Daughter 1: I think the fire alarm needs new batteries.

From Daughter 2: I cleaned the toilet, and we need more syrup.

From Daughter 1: Do I have to cook the macaroni & cheese before I eat it?

From Brian: Did you tell Daughter 2 she could go swimming naked?

From Daughter 2: Don't tell anyone, but I have got a daddy longlegs spider in my pocket.

From Brian: Where's your underwear?

From Daughter 1: I need the keys to the van.

From Daughter 2: I'm thinking about grilling some chicken. Can you start the grill for me?

From Daughter 1: I figured out why we need a lid on the popcorn when it's popping.

From Brian: Did we have five kids in the house when we went to sleep last night?

From Daughter 1: I need the area code for Hawaii.

From Daughter 2: What happens if the screwdriver goes down the toilet?

From Brian: What would you recommend to get paint off of the inside of dishwasher?

From Daughter 2: I might need a ladder. Do we have a ladder?

From Daughter 1: Can you wash curtains?

From Brian: I hope you weren't planning on showering today.

From Daughter 1: I can't get the couch cushion in the washing machine.

From Daughter 2: Can I have just one little wild pet in my room? You won't even know it's there.

From Brian: Feel like getting up anytime this afternoon?

The Ringing Of The Phone Prompts The Ringing In My Ears

The truth is that I, at one point in my life, had a social life. I had parties to attend every weekend. I had friends I could call on for shopping, dining, theatering (What!? It's totally a thing)... I had a wide and varied social circle. Then I had kids.

Please understand that it's not that my kids completely put a damper on my social life. It's just that with kids, who has the time? And, I'll argue that I still have a social life. Sorta.

Now, I maintain my friendships by visiting in line at Hellmart, emailing (and not just forwarding the Good Luck Buddha list from The Dalai Lama), and late night texting. I wish I could reach out and touch someone on the phone, but that doesn't work very well for me. Basically, I don't like talking on the phone.

I don't like talking on the phone at home for two reasons: 1) Daughter 1; and 2) Daughter 2.

What is it about the ring of a phone that causes my children (and children everywhere) to behave as Jodie Foster's Nell would behave upon first entering civilization? Is it the ringing? Is it one-sided conversation of which they are not a part? Is it the strange alignment of Venus with the moon during the fourth house of their birthdays?

I've spoken with enough other mommas out there to know that it's not just me. And if you listen very closely, you can hear *my* momma's voice saying, "It's paybacks, my dear!"

This afternoon, for example, I knew my friend Lori was going to call me as soon as her son was on the bus heading to school for afternoon kindergarten. I watched the clock closely and, when I knew little Ben was climbing on the bus in the wild, cold north, I started a movie for the daughters who happened to be home enjoying a snow day. I popped popcorn and presented them each with a big bowl of the buttery stuff and napkins. I prepared big glasses of water with straws. I got them each a blanket to have close by—just in case. I handed the volume remote to Daughter 1 and the DVD remote to Daughter 2, hoping to pre-empt any arguments between who had more control. I left no movie-need unmet.

The phone rang; I answered mid-first ring; I retreated to the other room. Ahhhh! A grown-up conversation with no interruptions.

"Hey, girl!" Lori started. "Is this a good time?"

"It's a great time," I whispered with my hand cupped over the phone so as to not let any noise tip off the daughters that I was on the phone. "The daughters are watching a movie and I'm ready to gab."

"Sounds great!" Lori commented. "What's new with you?"

Lori had barely gotten the sentiment stated and WHAM! I was knocked off the couch by a pillow. The curtains were somehow now off the rod. The couch had been moved to the middle of the room and fourteen quilts had been tossed over six dining room chairs to form a tent-like fort around me. All before I could tell her that I might be losing my ever-loving mind.

The Daughters had, in that exact moment, set up the karaoke machine and were singing along with Steppenwolf's "Magic Carpet Ride." They had found my make-up *and* perfume and were giving me a makeover while wearing dresses from my closet. Somehow they had found the Little Debbie snacks (the ones I hide for myself and only myself) and were chowin' down on Swiss Cake Rolls arguing over which one got the bigger twin-pack

Within thirty seconds, my phone conversation had been wrecked. I whimpered a good-bye to Lori and promised to call her as soon as they left for college (or a suitable boarding school).

I can hear dads everywhere asking why I don't have my conversations when the daughters are in bed or at least wait until Brian is home so he can help corral them. Don't think I haven't tried.

Oh! How I've tried! Don't. Think. I. Haven't. Tried.

A few nights earlier, I locked myself in the bathroom to have a conversation with my best friend from high school. Before I could even tell her the latest about our former Algebra II teacher (who was a mighty fine-looking girls' track coach from our junior year), the daughters had picked the lock and prepared a bubble bath, completely overflowing with bubbles and no less than twelve naked Barbies playing body-surfing-tidal-wave. My attentive hubby was watching an in-depth report on the fascinating subject of televised poker championships on *Outside the Lines* with a Thunder game on the picture-in-picture feature that only he knows how to work.

"What?" he said after pausing the TV.

My feet covered in bubbles and a Barbie in one hand, the phone in the other I commented, "What, indeed."

Honestly, I don't remember being this in-tune to telephone usage when I was a kid. If you listen very closely, that rumble you hear is my mother giggling—or crying, I can't tell which.

I do remember one time my mom was on the phone with a PTO lady planning the fall carnival and she handed me paper and pencil to keep me busy. I drew a picture of her with a tree in her forehead because when she wrinkled her face like that at me it did look like a tree was planted in her forehead. It alarmed her so much that she immediately got off the phone and rubbed in Oil of Old Lady for the rest of the afternoon. But, since she was off the phone, I had her make me some cookies. And pour me some milk.

There was another time that she was visiting on the phone with her sister in New Jersey. I wanted to carve our pumpkin for Halloween. Instead of disturbing her and asking her permission, I just got a knife myself and proceeded to slice open my finger. Wait now, I didn't *mean* to slice open my finger. That unfortunate incident just worked in my favor. I didn't *ask* her to get off the phone. She got off the phone all on her own. So she could tend to my bleeding. And drive me to the emergency room. So I could get three stitches in my finger. But, really, I wasn't *trying* to interrupt her.

If Miss America wants to really make the world a better place, she'd invent a ring that put children to sleep at its initial sound. There's a technological challenge for Bill Gates. There's nothing more satisfying than being able to start and finish a conversation without interruption by fighting, screaming, singing or bleeding.

I'm fairly certain that the problems in the Middle East could have been worked out already by now if the children of the leaders hadn't heard the phone ring when the peace treaty call came in.

Minivans Are Not A Curse

Brian recently changed jobs and is now driving quite a bit more than he used to drive. So when the government announced a fun little program called "Cash for Clunkers," we turned into Cuba Gooding Jr. and began yelling, "Show me the money!"

Brian drove a twelve-year old truck. It was the epitome of a clunker. Best-case scenario: the blue book had us paying about $50 to have it towed off. There was NO way we were even going to get some little 17-year-old to spend even half of his Burger King paycheck on it as his first vehicle. Cash for Clunkers was certainly the deal for us. And wasn't it our patriotic duty to boost the economy? At least that's what Brian's poker pals told him to tell me. I'll admit: I bought into their little economic plan.

Brian had my blessing to go find himself a car. Now, before you start dissecting that sentence trying to figure out the dynamics of our relationship, I have to fill you in about a deal Brian and I made with each other even before we were married: I will never meddle in his buying a vehicle if he will never buy a vehicle just "for fun."

That's right: Brian likes to negotiate and if I don't keep a tight reign on him on a Saturday afternoon, he'd buy a car—but it would be a good deal. And boy would it be fun.

I, on the other hand, can't stand to go car shopping.

If I like the salesman, then I immediately picture his four, hungry children at home (with a crop in the field?) waiting on their daddy to make a deal so he can go buy them some of the blue-box macaroni and cheese with the foil-pouched, liquid cheese (no more store brand!) because it will be a banner day at their home with their daddy's commission check! If I don't like the salesman, I won't even talk to him. At all. And I imagine him selling just one more car to support his Ecstasy habit and leaving before we've even start the car to drive it off the lot to go par-tay with his frat brothers at Hooters. WOO!

Either way, I am very nervous even standing on the lot. I feel like someone in some car-office somewhere has his sights set on me and they can see what the rest of the world can't: a very faint "Sucker" written on my forehead.

Brian, however, *lives* to make deals. He *loves* to go for a test drive and then just "chat" with the salesman. "Just talking. That's all." Those words almost bought me a GMC Jimmy on our third date when he said, "Wouldn't it be fun to go test drive a car?" And I said, "[giggle, giggle] Sure." (I was very giggly on our third through seventh dates.) One thirty-minute test drive and a twenty-minute negotiation later, I realized that we might be buying a car together … I hadn't even seen his underwear yet. I began sweating profusely and hyperventilating and Brian said, "We'll think about it" and we walked out. On our way to the movies (our real date for the night), he turned to me and said, "That was fun, huh?" It was at *that* moment that I realized he'd be the negotiator of "us" if I survived to the point of "us" without going into cardiac arrest.

So Brian picked out an SUV, called me to get the OK as far as our family was concerned, and I told him to get it—apparently, with Cash for Clunkers, everyone else picked out the exact same car. We spent the last three weeks of the Cash for Clunkers deal chasing down this elusive vehicle, driving over five hundred miles in every direction to various dealers who promised to have one waiting on their lot by the time we pulled in. We were doing nothing more than snipe hunting for an Equinox.

I finally suggested that he maybe could try a minivan—they're literally everywhere. He liked driving my minivan, after all. But, he said that he felt like it would be overkill for our family to have *two* minivans. "Besides," he said, "I'm cooler than that." I asked him if his poker pals thought it was cool to sleep on the couch like he was going to be doing! I kid. He'll sleep on the recliner. It fits his tall frame better.

Eventually, we found the SUV for us and Brian (who really is very considerate) wanted me to go check it out before he actually signed on the dotted line. He negotiated without me present—that way, we wouldn't need a paramedic on hand. And I went to check out his new set of wheels.

I had no idea what I was looking for or looking at. There was a CD player. Great. A light for the mirror (driver's *and* passenger's side), and four wheels. Looks good to me.

But I didn't want to feel like an idiot, so I asked if they happened to sell "New Car Smell" in a spray bottle because I'd pay full price for that. Brian smiled at the salesman and explained, "She drives a minivan." The salesman nodded and sighed an all-knowing "Ahhh …"

I'll bet that salesman spends a lot of nights in his recliner, too.

Socks Will Be The End Of The World

Because I'm a little bit on the "Type A" side (some might even call me anal but I wouldn't go quite that far), I like to do my laundry all on one day. Since I work outside of my home full time, this means that the most logical day for me to do all the laundry all at one time would be Saturday.

I hear ya and I have no idea why I torture myself in this way.

And because I'm a little bit (a lotta bit?) on the analytical side, I like to finish my laundry all on one day. I like to leave no dirty clothing item unsudsed, unfluffed or unfolded. [Editor's note: proof that there is no such thing as "a little bit type A."]

The part of laundry I don't like—no way, no how—is the socks. How in the WORLD can a family of four produce no less than 297 individual socks in a week? Sock sorting and matching really could be a full-time job in and of itself, and I wish it would be a full time job that we could outsource; but, alas, sock sorters are few and far between.

One Saturday, Brian became my knight in striped tube socks.

In an effort to redeem himself for letting the nacho-cheese caked crock-pot soak in the sink for four days after his monthly poker night, Brian decided he'd help me out by sorting and matching and folding the mountain of socks that had accumulated. In return, I'd wear that cute little lacy red thing to bed. Seemed totally fair to me.

I walked through the living room to find him, laundry basket in lap, watching Comedy Central and sorting socks. I stopped, wiped a tear from the corner of my eye and made the "I Love You" sign to him as I was too choked to speak.

Brian winked and said, "Anything for you, honey, and the cute little lacy red thing!"

I got a drink in the kitchen and came back through the living room to find the basket sitting at the foot of the recliner and the remote already in his hand. He was—shocker!—flipping channels.

"Honey? Why'd you stop?" I ask in my sweet voice.

"Stop what? That channel? Commercial."

"No. Why'd you stop with the socks?"

"Done."

Done. Done? In a matter of maybe ninety seconds he was done?

Seeing my quizzical look, he hopped up real quick like, grabbed the basket and proceeded to put them in the drawers! Hired! He was hired to be the full-time sock boy—excuse me, *man*. I was going to call him sock puppet, but I think he'd see right through that touch of sarcasm.

By Sunday morning after church when I was changing into comfy clothes, and tossing the red lacy thing into the dirty clothes hamper before The Daughters found it and played dress up, I realized how he had been such a whiz at sock sorting: it was because he didn't. He didn't sort the socks at all. It seemed that he just skipped right over the sorting part of sock sorting. As I pulled out a big pair of white tube socks-perfect for lounging around the house on a winter's day with my pajama pants and sweat top, I realized that I didn't have a *pair* of white tube socks. I had a white tube sock and a pink bobbin sock, which was fourteen sizes too small for me.

"Honey!" I said in my sweet voice again, "These socks don't match."

Quick as you can say "red little lacy thing," he assured me that it must have been a one-time mess up and hurriedly found me a matching pair of socks.

Daughter 1, who takes after her momma in that she's a very organized, precise person (read: anal and obsessive), came crying from her room! NONE of her socks matched. Because of this, she had to undo ALL of her socks. What was she to do now that she had 85 socks, unmatched, on her bedroom floor?

Gee, I don't know … Match them up???

"MOMMA! Gah!" All the organization and precision in the world can't make up for her lack of recognizing the glaringly obvious.

"Honey!" I said in my not-so-sweet voice, "ALL of Daughter 1's socks don't match."

"Weird," Brian replied. And frantically changed channels.

Weird indeed.

Daughter 2, who is more like Brian in that they are both more laid back and obviously don't care that things that match should, in fact, be matched up, emerged from her room wearing one of my trouser socks pulled up over her knee and a Dora sock that she last wore sometime in her first year of life. She also had on flip-flops, but that's a different story.

I was very quick to remind Brian that Saturday was laundry day and now it was Sunday and I was going to be doing sock sorting *all day long* because he didn't do it right the first time.

Brian, a smart and sneaky man, was hurt. His face showed his angst from his furrowed brow to his pouty bottom lip and quivering chin. Whatever. I would not give in to his forced emotion.

"Fine," Brian whispered, "I was just trying to help, but I guess I didn't do it right. I won't help you with the socks again!"

"Thank you …" I muttered.

Wait …

Was that a slight grin at the corners of his pouting lips? Was he really hanging his head in shame or was he trying to hide the look of triumph on his face. Did I really just thank him for offering to not help with laundry again? Oh. No.

But don't worry about me. I took the batteries out of the remote until the socks were indeed matched. And I banned nacho cheese from any subsequent poker nights, unless a fellow Momma out there needs her socks sorted on poker weekend.

Coming Out Of The ~~Closet~~ Tunnel

When I was in first grade, my elementary school had those cement "tunnels." These tunnels, I'm sure, were not purchased from a playground equipment catalog, but rather from a construction or industrial equipment catalog, and they had something to do with drainage. Regardless of where the two tunnels were purchased, we loved them. Like first graders everywhere, we lived and breathed rules. And the first rule was that one tunnel was for boys only and the other was for girls only.

Unless (there's always an *unless* and it's always italicized) a boy chased a girl and caught her. Then he would put the girl in the boy tunnel and stand guard at one end of the tunnel. The girl would then crawl out of the other end, stand with her hands on her hips, stick out her tongue and take off running as the chase began yet again.

Pretty much, I left the boys alone.

I had no interest in running.

When the boys weren't chasing girls, they played with their Matchbox cars and I really had no interest in Matchbox cars either.

One crisp fall day, though, curiosity got the best of me. I wanted to know what was in the boy tunnel. Was there a big deer head and perhaps some mismatched leather chairs? Was there a black velvet painting of a girl stretched out over the hood of a Trans Am? I needed to know. I worked up the courage and stood over the boys as they raced around their pea-gravel track, and I dropped an acorn right in the path of Peter Paul Woodyer's yellow car. Peter Paul stood up, and the chase was on, with me screaming all the way. As I rounded the jungle gym for the twelfth time, I remembered the whole reason I wanted Peter Paul to take chase was so that he would put me in the boy tunnel. So, I stopped. I turned and faced Peter Paul and said, "Fine. Put me in the boy tunnel." It was the first and last time I was directly blunt with a boy.

Peter Paul, who I'm pretty sure thought I was hot stuff because I caught him raising my skirt one day to look at my panties, said, "No." I begged him until he finally agreed.

Yes! I was going in. Once inside the tunnel, I saw that pretty much it was the same as the girl tunnel with one exception: Someone had smuggled a piece of chalk into the tunnel and drawn a picture of a naked woman—complete with little ruffles between her legs, whatever that was. And the artist had written "F*** ME" right above the picture. I know for a fact that those were the words because I was in the redbird reading group, and we were the best.

That night, when my mom was sitting on the toilet, which was where most of our intimate conversations took place, I asked my mom was F*** meant. She told me it wasn't nice. I said, "OK, but what does it mean?"

"Well, it's just a very nice word."

"And F*** means … what?" I was nothing if not insistent.

"OK, it's when a boy puts something of his in your private area. It's not very nice. Please don't say it again."

"What does he put there?" I persisted.

Sparing no detail, she began to explain. It started with "Well, you have a vagina …"

At this point, I am pretty sure I tuned her out; she may have been very explicit, but what I got from the entire conversation was that boys put something of theirs that only they have in my private area. That's what F*** meant. Got it.

The next day at school, I was so ready to use my new vocabulary word. At recess, I saw the boys playing with their Matchbox cars, *which I didn't have*—only boys had, and I dropped acorns on top of their cars and took off running. Not only did Peter Paul begin to chase me. *All* the boys began to chase me. They grabbed up their cars and came barreling after me. Oh no. This was it. They had their Matchbox cars and were chasing after me. This only meant one thing. They not only planned to put me in the tunnel; they planned to F*** me. Here was my chance: I sucked in my breath and belted out as loud as I could, "Don't F*** me!" Then I yelled it again. And again. And again. And again until the recess teacher stopped me and dragged my little foul-mouthed self to the office.

That night, while not sitting on the toilet, my mom explained—using correct terminology and everything!—exactly what was involved in sexual intercourse between a man and a woman. I was 7 years old and it scared me.

I remember thinking that I would much rather have a Matchbox car in my private area than a penis in my vagina. I wasn't even certain that I had a vagina — that night in the bathtub, however, I was able to confirm that I did, indeed, have an extra hole down there.

Damn, my mom was smart.

"Someone Stop The Bleeding!"

After enduring my own childhood and very bumpy adolescence, I found myself in very precarious position when Daughter 1 was asking all sorts of questions about her own personal development. She didn't ask what F*** meant as I had when I was her age, but I knew it was coming. I didn't want to prejudice her against Matchbox cars, but I did want her to have good information. So, I decided to take the chicken way out and buy a book.

One Saturday night, while Brian and his bros were playing poker in the living room, Daughter 1 and I were lying in bed with the latest version of the *Know Your Body* book. The one thing I can say for certain about Daughter 1 is that she loves her books. So, without much discussion, she said she'd love to read the book, and she promised to come to me with any questions she may have.

"Do you want me to read with you?" I offered lovingly to my first born, who may or may not have been on the threshold of womanhood.

"Well, Momma, you read kinda of choppy and your breath stinks, so I think I'll just read on my own." With that, I crawled from her bed and wiped a tear from my eye and the sweat from my brow and heaved a big ol' sigh of relief as I skipped off to brush my teeth.

The next afternoon, Daughter 2 came running into me as I was standing at the stove sautéing onions hoping to give the illusion that I was doing more than reheating last night's lasagna. "Momma!! How do I stop the bleeding??"

"OHMYGOSH! Who's bleeding?" I gasped.

"ME!" She screamed

I grabbed her by the shoulders and knelt down beside her, "Where?" I screamed back.

"Well, not now!" she sobbed. "But, Daughter 1 told me that I would start randomly bleeding from my bottom and then I'd have to wear a tampon and then I have to have a baby! I'm too young to bleed and have a baby!"

Okay. So maybe Daughter 1 needed some help reading—or at least interpreting—after all. We sat down, Momma and Daughter, and decided that before she discussed bleeding or any other fun piece of information with her sister or anyone else, she was to talk about it with me first. And, on the off chance that she had a question and I was not available (When would this be? I teach at her school.), she could ask her daddy.

In retrospect, maybe I should have tipped Brian off that Daughter 1 was reading her way through puberty, but I think it was pretty fun with him caught completely off-guard. And by completely off-guard, I mean that he had no clue what Daughter 1 meant when she stood in front of him as he watched *SportsCenter*, removed her shirt and asked him what stage he thought her breasts were in. I reminded him that when he was 12 years old, he probably wished upon a star that a girl would ask him to stare at her boobs, so this was really all his fault.

Nevertheless, Daughter 1 explained the four stages of breast development to him: 1. Flat as the Kansas plains; 2. Bumps in the road; 3. Molehills wishing to be mountains; and 4. The Grand Tetons. They decided together that she was clearly in stage two. I came home to find Brian barricaded in our bedroom by himself and Daughter 1 playing the Wii topless — "letting the breasts breath a little."

Later on that week, she popped into the shower with me one morning. This is not an uncommon occurrence as she's learned that getting in the shower with me in the mornings that she pretty much has my undivided attention because … where am I going to go? But she joined me as I was shaving my pits (the things I do for love) and declared that I was in stage three. "Do you think you'll ever get to stage four, Momma?" I assured her that if her daddy ever won the lottery, I'd probably be at a stage four in two to three days, depending on the recovery time.

Then I got out of the shower, dried myself and my stage three floppies and hid the damn book. At this point, I'm convinced it'd be much easier, and certainly much more relieving to the family, to just let her be afraid of Matchbox cars.

An Ill-Prepared Family Drip Dries

A while back, I left Brian and the daughters home alone as I attended an overnight conference. At 5:30 that morning as I was quietly getting ready to leave, I noticed that one of our bathrooms was completely out of toilet paper. I reached above the toilet to grab a new roll and it was completely out. I hurried to the Toilet Paper Command Center (also known as the hall closet) and removed the last roll of toilet paper in the house.

I know! My heart is racing just thinking about being out of the stuff! My heart is also racing because if Brian ever lets us get this close to being out of toilet paper, I'd consider it grounds for legal action.

Hurriedly, I raced to the other bathrooms and discovered that they, too, were out of extra toilet paper and their on-roll supply was at about half!

My first feeling was of failure: How in the world could I let my house exist in this kind of disorganization? This kind of disarray? This kind of disparity? I was expected to leave the house in ten minutes! There was no way I could run to Hellmart and restock before having to leave their tiny hineys to such limited resources!

My second feeling was of quasi-relief: Brian is a resourceful man. He could go buy the toilet paper himself, right? RIGHT? (I'm looking for confirmation here, people!)

My third feeling was of hilarity: Brian would never notice the lack of toilet paper anywhere in the house until he sat down to take his six o'clock poop. Yes, he really is that much of a regular guy.

At this point, it was too late. I had to go. I would wake Brian and command him to, as wives and mothers in San Antonio did in the days of yore, "Remember the toilet paper!"

"Bubby," I whispered. "We're out of toilet paper."

"It's a double play! I'm up to bat," he grumbled back.

"No. Listen to me!" I said a bit louder shaking him in his dream-filled state. "We have no more extra rolls of toilet paper in the house."

He barely opened his eyes.

"Do you understand what this means?" I demanded. "You'll have to go buy some. Go buy your family toilet paper."

Then his eyes closed. And all I could do was pray that he remembered my message. And that he got a homerun.

For the entirety of my conference trip, I thought about my stranded family. While my fellow-conference goers and I were shopping, I sent powerful thought-waves to Brian to go get some TP. While we were eating and dancing at Joe's Crab Shack, I hoped beyond hope that he'd remember the two-ply. While we were sitting in the hotel hot tub with a hot Marine, I considered texting him and reminding him to stock-up on the necessary, little rolls of heaven. Oh, it was but a fleeing consideration ... didn't you just read? Hot. Marine.

Finally, the conference was concluded and I was on my way home. At bedtime that evening, I walked through my door and headed straight to the bathroom. I needed reassurance that Brian and I had shared a toilet-paper telepathy. And I had just driven three hours with a

64-ounce drink.

That toilet paper was sitting at half roll with no extras. Upon completion, I hurried to the next restroom, and that toilet paper was completely out ... with no spare above the cabinet. I dashed to the first throne and found absolutely no sign of toilet paper anywhere ... not even on the spinner-dealie.

Frantically and breathlessly, I opened the toilet paper closet and found it to be empty, too. I hung my head. I had failed as a Momma to keep the house stocked of the most important, most essential staple. I had left my family in despair as a result of this failure.

Brian appeared at my side. He felt my sense of doom. He acknowledged my hurt and decided to encourage me.

He gently slipped his arm around my hunkered-down shoulders. "Honey," he whispered, "It's alright. We didn't need that much toilet paper."

I looked up at his resourceful, economical and obviously environmentally friendly face through my bloodshot eyes. (What? We were in the hot tub for a long time. Let me say this again: Hot. Marine. We were in the hot tub for a very, very long time.)

"I let the daughters go outside!" What was he saying? They can go outside anytime they want. I shook my head at him to indicate that I didn't get what he meant when he said he let the daughters *go* outside. Oh. *Go.* Nice. My sweet, innocent daughters had learned the finer art of peeing outside. I only hope they were confined to the back yard.

Unsupervised Child: A Real-Life Home Alone Story

If I were ever graced with any alone time at my own home, you'd experience the sigh heard 'round the world, right before I stretched across the entire bed and snoozed. For a week solid.

No … No time alone for me. See, Daughter 1 has been sick yet again. Honestly, I'm surprised I'm not sick more often. Hell!—I'm surprised I am any kind of well at all. I work around kids all day. I drive to and from work with my own two kids. At least one of them will crawl into bed with Brian and me each night. I get no alone time. I'm afraid if I were to get sick, I'd probably come down with pneumonia-strep-bacterial-itis. I'm sure it exists. Trust me.

Anyway, Daughter 1 woke me up about midnight telling me that her tummy hurt and that she had already sat on the toilet for precisely twenty-four minutes (she's a bit obsessive like that, so I believe she really did). Nothing was helping. I told her to get a wet rag (a cure-all, am I right?) and put it on her head once she was laying back in her own quiet bedroom in a bed that I was not also laying in.

"Alright, Momma," she softly and sweetly agreed right before she puked all over me. Quickly, we got cleaned up and retreated to the sick chair to watch some late-night Olympics (late-night TV, another cure-all). Every half-hour, we'd race to the bathroom. This went on for hours. All. Night. Long.

Brian-who can hear me whispering about a girls-night-out plan from the garage —slept through the entire adventure, waking at six and wanting to know what was going on. Daughter 1 had finally dozed off. Exhausted, I headed back to bed and mumbled instructions for him to wake me when he left for work.

When he left, I mumbled for him to call me every thirty minutes until I was awake so I could take Daughter 2 to school.

Of course, on his way to work, his phone lost service, dropped calls, drove by a secret government alien landing site. Whatever. The point is, I got no more calls. And so, I slept.

About fifteen minutes before Daughter 2 had to be at school, Daughter 1 woke me up because she was throwing up again. Daughter 2 was back in bed asleep. School is about twelve minutes away. I hollered for Daughter 2 to wake up, as I sat Daughter 1 on the toilet with her throw-up tub; tossed Daughter 2 a cereal bar for breakfast and sprinted to the van in my lovely blue plaid pajama top, my black spotted pajama bottoms and my copper-and-beige mules. I was a lovely sight. I quickly tossed in the snacks for Daughter 2's class (that I had forgotten to take to school on Monday) and off we sped toward school.

With Daughter 1 still sitting on the toilet at home.

That's right. It was a real-life Macaulay Caulken movie.

Only, I was not in Paris—France OR Texas—though either one would have been a pleasant little escape.

I decided that Daughter 1, while only 8 years old at the time, was very mature and could handle it and would realize that the rapture hadn't come and she hadn't been left behind by anyone but her very tired momma.

I squealed into the school parking lot, slid the van door open and pushed Daughter 2 out, who enlisted the help of Emma's dad to help her carry all of her stuff into her room, since I had pushed it out right on top of her. She was at least on school grounds. Set the bar low, that's my mothering motto.

As soon as I saw Daughter 2 struggle and fall into the classroom door, I NASCAR-ed the van back toward home. [Note from my editor: *I'm embarrassed that I know that NASCAR is an acronym.*] [Note from me: *It's alright. I love you anyway.*]

At the first stop sign, I noticed that the tires sounded different when I paused (notice I didn't say "stop"—let's just let that one "slide," if ya know what I mean). I thought about calling Brian and reporting weird tire sounds when I discovered that I didn't have my phone with me. This caused me to feel great concern and relief at the exact same time. At least Daughter 1 had my phone at home in case there was an emergency; however, if she thought being left home alone—sick and on the toilet—was indeed an emergency, then I'd have a lot of explaining to do to the nice police officers that may or may not be waiting for me at my house.

When I turned onto the main road away from school and back toward the house, the tire noise got louder and weirder. I'd never heard this sound before. I slowed down and the noise slowed down. I sped up and the noise sped up. Really: With a sick child at home, I didn't have time to deal with tires.

I glanced toward the back of the van only to discover that … the van door was still open.

This has only happened to me once before (that I'll admit to!) Right after Daughter 2 was born, my mother was convinced that I was not capable of navigating Hellmart and two kids at the same time. So, as soon as she left town for a cruise, I packed up Daughter 1, who was 2 years old at the time, and a three-week old Daughter 2 and headed to Hellmart, just to show my own momma that I could handle myself.

As we pulled away from the house, Daughter 1 said, "This is fun! I'm gonna tell Nana."

I said, "That's right, Baby Girl. You tell your Nana that your Momma took you *and* your sister out and we all survived and even had fun!"

"Yes!" giggled Daughter 1, "Nana never lets us ride in the van with the door open!" OK, so we didn't tell Nana that part.

But I digress. I immediately pulled over, shut the door and continued my speed-qualifying drive home. I pulled in hot and ran into the house to discover a naked Daughter 1, who had started a load of laundry ("because there are germs on that old pair of pajamas"), watching everyone's favorite feel-good show, *Phineas and Ferb*.

Not once did she mention my hasty retreat, leaving her fending for her sick self. Not once did she use my phone to call 911, the neighbors, her friends or even her Nana. The house was not on fire nor was it flooded. And, actually, I'm not even sure she realized I was gone.

Please, don't call Child Services; I am fully aware that she's still much too young to stay home alone, but it's good to know that she'd be alright if it were an emergency situation. It makes a momma proud.

So proud, that I'm gonna celebrate with an emergency pedicure. Don't worry. I'll be sure to take my phone with me.

Itty Bitty Titty Committee

I "developed" early as a young woman. I got my first bra (and not of the training variety, either) when I was in fourth grade. And I peaked (no pun intended—well, maybe just a little pun) in the fifth grade. I am not, as they like to say, "blessed in the chest." Really, I have no idea who says that. Maybe it will catch on.

So when a friend suggested that we go get properly sized for a bra a few years back, I screamed, "Hell to the NO!" right in her face. No, I didn't really scream in her face as she emailed me her idea first, so I screamed at the computer. At work. People rarely bother me anymore when I'm sitting at the computer.

After screaming at the computer and then composing myself, I agreed to go with her. Because I like being told that I look like a fifth grader, developmentally speaking.

Truth be told, the very first time I was fitted for a bra was when I was eight months pregnant with Daughter 1. I was in the market for a nursing bra, of course. I walked into the store at the mall an excited, tired momma-to-be, feeling like I was carrying around a gallon of sour cream in each ta-ta. The perky (another pun intended) size two "mommy's helper" measured me, and then announced my size.

Math's never been a strong suit for me, but it didn't really take long for me to do two things: 1. Figure out that I had lost (yes, I said *lost*) an inch and (yes, I said *and*) a cup size; and 2. Kick Miss Hooters right in the shins. Hormones will make you do some wild things, I tell ya.

I was devastated to find out that my pregnancy boobs were on backorder … and, now that I think about it, I never even got them. Brian was sympathetic to this plight as well. Or maybe he was sympathetic to his plight of his wife not getting a boost of endowment after eight months of pregnancy hormones.

The Daughters are now schoolgirls, themselves. I never did get any additional boobage from my pregnancies, but mommahood sure had changed my cleavage (or lack thereof), so I consented to go with my friend to be properly fitted. Who knows? It might be fun. Like going-to-the-mall-on-a-Friday-night-when-the-football-team-is-out-of-town-and-every-stinkin'-14-year-old-is-also-at-the-mall is fun!

The first thing I noticed when my friend picked me up was that she was very blessed in the chest. (Look! It's already catching on.) I hung my head in shame. She, however, did not have a minivan. And this just goes to show that you can't have it all.

We arrived at the official measuring station and someone resembling my great grandmother stepped out from behind her desk and led us to the dressing room where we disrobed from the waist up and slipped on a silky, pillowcase-type top. Then Granny and her friend, Miss Elmira Gulch (you know her from *The Wizard of Oz*, riding a bike, cackling something about getting a little dog … really, I swear it was her) met us in our individual rooms.

First off, we had to report our current bra size, so that they could record it for the official measuring paper. Then the measuring began. Lucky me, Miss Elmira

Gulch was going to be my official fitter. Elmira said not one word as she measured over and under and around and top to bottom and side to side. At one point, I completely felt like I had been just a tab bit unfaithful to Brian.

Then she went and got her calculator. Calculator? Really? What kind of Professional Cleavage Connoisseur needs a calculator?

While she was gone, I heard my friend and Granny chatting it up and laughing like long lost bosom buddies. I wished that I had Granny measuring me. I also wished for bigger ta-tas. Maybe that's why Elmira needed the calculator. Maybe I just was coming into my own later on in life … like twenty-five years after fifth grade.

Elmira returned and told me that I must have told her the wrong bra size. I quickly grabbed my bra and glanced again at the size then showed it to The Wicked Witch of the West who pronounced that I had been wearing the wrong size after all.

Of course I had. Here comes the hard-core, high-pressure sales to get me to buy one of their bras in my hard-to-find size, right? I had grown-I just knew it.

"You're not a C cup." I smiled. Of course, I wasn't. I, and my knockers, were moving on up in the world. "You're a B," she cackled. I explained to her that I had been counting calories and—lucky me!—it was paying off. She cackled again.

I threw my cup of ice water on her. When she didn't melt, I just knew that flying monkeys were going to descend upon me, chanting, "Itty, Bitty, Titty Committee." You remember the chant, right? But, no need to relive seventh grade right now.

Elmira dabbed off her face with my grossly oversized boulder-holder and assured me that they had plenty of padded brassieres that would, indeed, make mountains out of my molehills.

At that same time, my friend emerged from her room beaming like proud mother at a dance recital: "I'm an F cup!" she cheered.

I couldn't stand it anymore. I threw my water on her and screamed, "I'll show you F cup."

Security kindly let me retrieve my damp bra and blouse before escorting me from the store. Elmira threw a pair of socks at me on my way out. I couldn't quite understand what she said, but it sounded a little bit like she said, "Stuff it."

An Empty Can Is A Sign Of A Lazy Husband

Back when Brian was just The Boyfriend, we went to his hometown to meet his family. While we were there, his momma cooked a full meal and invited all of the aunts, uncles, cousins and grandmas who could be found. Before we sat down to eat, Brian's momma said to her grown son, "Take out this trash."

And Brian grabbed a trash bag-nay, several trash bags--and proceeded to empty the trash and replace the liner of *all* the trashcans in the home not just the specific trashcan that his momma originally referred to.

Now, I will admit that at the time, I really liked Brian. A lot. But, this totally sealed the deal for me. I got misty eyed and started naming children that my loins would bear for the man who not only emptied the trash but also replaced the liner. And he did it when he was asked to! Ladies, I had found the perfect man.

Keyword here: *found.* This is past tense for *did find but can find no more*.

Fast forward six months later (or any given day since then). We're now married. I ask Brian to take out the trash. Sadly, however, I was a bit astonished to learn that we left off the "take the trash out" part of our wedding vows.

Please understand: it's not that he doesn't take the trash out. He does. On occasion. If I don't beat him to it. Truth is, if I see the trash needs to be taken out, I do something about it. Ah, hellz no, I don't take it out myself. I smoosh it down with my foot or a broom. Then I pile on some more until it can be smooshed no more. THEN, I ask Brian to take the trash out.

After ten minutes, I attempt to smoosh some more. And I gently remind him, "Hon! I really need you to take out the trash!"

Then, after fifteen more minutes, I start piling next to it and I remind Brian to take it out with just a touch of stern-ness to my voice, "Hey, Mister! The Trash! Pronto!"

After a total of thirty minutes (give or take three hours), I stomp and huff and screech until finally he pauses the TV on C-Span to make it look like he's being torn from something massively important, when I know for a fact that thirty seconds earlier he was watching and re-watching the Shake-Weight infomercial. Once he takes the trash out, he'll resume his seat catching up on the latest financial escapades of the contact-lens lobbyists. Right.

So, I load my arms with the latest hunks of junk only to drop them at my feet so that I can reach, right above the trashcan, and replace the liner. When Brian hears the sighs and the mumbles of do-it-yourself vasectomies, he jumps from the recliner and takes the rest of the trash from the house and then hides himself in the backyard with his MP3 player.

I hear ya and you're right: I could gently remind him and wait for him to do it at his leisure. BWAHAhahahahaha! And then we could go on that TV show where the people come and scrape the garbage into a big bin in the front yard using small bulldozers.

Sure, I suppose I could just take it out myself. But

then what would I have to gripe about?

I could compromise and let him take out the trash and I put in the liner ... but remind me sometime to tell you how that whole, "You cook and I'll clean, honey" compromise worked out for us.

Until then, I'll keep the laptop open to my Google search of "At-home vasectomies." It's working so far.

Another job that strictly belongs to Brian is his annual hunting trip. The beauty of this hunting trip is that he never has to leave home. Yes, we do live in town. No, the hunting trip doesn't involve live ammo. Yes, I'm talking about hunting down mice … Like Tom the cat hunts down Jerry the cartoon character … only funnier.

As often happens during the winter, critters move inside. And our house may as well have a flashing *Vacancy* sign over the roof. All winter long, we've shared our house with a mouse. A pregnant mouse. We know she was pregnant because about a week after we discovered she had eaten through a half of a loaf of bread, we discovered her babies.

The daughters were very generous—albeit unknowingly—and fed the little mouse family with their crumbs and morsels and crusts that they tossed behind the couch when they weren't even supposed to be eating in the living room in the first place.

But I digress.

Initially, Brian and I were humane about their departures, then the little varmints ate through an entire package of Brian's peanut butter cookies and the game was on.

One by one, Brian delighted in his mouse disposal and slowly we regained control of our grain products. Or so we thought.

One morning, we awoke to a half-eaten English muffin and evidence that the lone remaining mouse was still alive and … um, regular. Brian mumbled a few choice words and the hunt was on. Again.

This last mouse, however, was a slippery little devil. It would eat the hot dog buns in the breadbasket, the crackers in the box on top of the microwave and the peanut butter off the trap. It was a taunting thief to Brian's keystone cop.

One evening, I noticed Brian slathering camo make-up on his face.

"What are you doing?" I asked him.

"You can't handle the truth!" he shouted at me, then he crouched in the corner of the kitchen and muttered, "I love the smell of canned cheese in the morning."

I heard a little high-pitched snickering coming from behind the fridge and saw a slinky little tail shake.

A few days went by and we hadn't seen any evidence of our furry little boarder. Of course, we had placed every morsel of food we had in a metal footlocker that Brian found at the military booth down at the flea market. We thought we had starved the little carb-addict out, and he'd moved to the house next door.

We were wrong.

The next night, Mighty Mouse made his boldest appearance ever. While Brian and I were having a *Twilight* marathon on DVD … Wait; Brian asked me to say it like this: *While I was watching* Twilight *and Brian was reading* Sports Illustrated, the little hair ball moseyed right into the living room and paused in front of the TV. (Edited to add, again: Brian was NOT watching *Twilight.* In particular, he was not watching *Eclipse.* He does not watch such mush; however, he does have a very distinct opinion on why Bella should grant Edward his wish and not become a vampire until after they are married. Let's be very clear on that point.)

Since I, too, have very strong opinions about Edward and Bella's relationship, I was totally engrossed in the show and didn't notice the little creature feature teasing Brian. Later, Brian would say that he swore the rodent said, "Wussies watch vampire flicks."

Without any warning, Brian threw the remote in the general direction of the TV and shouted, a la William Wallace, "Freedom!" Then he bounded from the recliner and dove under the entertainment center. He hastily grabbed a shoe that Daughter 2 left in the living room because she thinks the whole house is her shoebox and slammed the shoe onto the floor behind the TV. Then he jumped up onto the mantle, all the while wildly swinging the karaoke microphone. When the cord from the microphone went tight, he rounded the corner into the front room and grabbed the quilt off the wall, slamming it down and sliding under the dining room table. He eventually emerged holding a chair in the style of a lion tamer and ran into kitchen screaming, "I've got him now!"

Still. I had no idea he had even seen a mouse. I was poised to call 9-1-1 and request the loony bin send a wagon right on over to Bedlam, via our house when I heard S N A P. The trap had been sprung. At that point, I realized that Brian had apparently been warring with the mouse. And the war was over.

Then the screaming began.

It seems that our little mouse had played Brian just as Road Runner played Coyote. Somehow, our mouse had finagled Brian's heel right into the trap. Neither man, nor mouse, was injured—very much.

But The Daughters do wonder why Brian has moved the refrigerator to the middle of the kitchen and is crouched in its place mumbling, "Be vewwy, vewwy quiet! I'm hunting!"

Actual Things I Have Pulled Out Of Our Trash Before They Made It To The Curb

- An entire bottle of cough syrup
- A school backpack with homework still in it
- My "Hide-the-veggies-in-the-mac-and-cheese" cookbook
- A cowboy hat
- Two beach towels
- Three frogs (alive)
- Five Barbie legs and three Barbie arms
- High-heeled boots that fit no one in our family
- A three-inch pony tail (the exact color of Daughter 1's hair)
- Three plastic containers with Daughter 2's lunch still in them.
- A box of trash liners
- Two cans of spinach
- A bottle of coconut-scented shampoo
- My healthy cooking magazines
- A box of prunes
- Three completely full containers of dental floss
- Subtraction flashcards
- An entire box of 24 crayons, with each and every crayon broken in half

Angelina Jolie's Lips Are Not For Sissies

I am not a morning person. I will be the first (in a long line of people, including Brian, the daughters, my mom, my sister, college roommates, middle school sleepover attendees, cabins full of church campers) to admit that I just do *not* do mornings. Because school does, indeed, start in the morning, and I am not only a teacher but I have the daughters to get to school in the mornings, then I must *endure* the mornings. When I have to. It wouldn't hurt my feelings one bit, however, to never have to wake up before 11:00am for the rest of my life.

With all that being said, I am always looking for ways to save time in the mornings, thus allowing me to hit snooze nine times instead of seven (or eight if I'm feeling lucky!). You know—things like shaving (only on days when the hemline comes close to my knee and then only if it's been longer than a week since I shaved last), cooking breakfast (What? Fiber One bars are healthy, require no cooking and are easily caught as I'm tossing them to The Daughters on our mad dash to the minivan.), ironing clothes (Simple—wrinkled is in … plus, you just might make the back page of *Glamour* magazine, as a DON'T.).

Shhh. If you listen really well, you can hear my mother whimper because I don't iron. My doctor said that there is such a thing as too much iron and I always do what my doctor says.

Let's continue shall we?

As I was saying, morning comes way too early for me. So when my favorite aunt took a course to become an Aesthetic Beautician for Permanent Cosmetics (Read: tattoo artist for lips and eyes for the rich but trashy woman) and offered to give me "permanent make up," I raced right on down to Dallas to have my lips and my eyes done. That would, after all, save five minutes in my morning not having to put on make up. And that, my friends, is equivalent to one extra snooze. And extra snoozes are nothing to sneeze at.

My cousin had recently had her lips done by my aunt and said that the first pass with the needle was the worst. After that the numbing solution kicks in and the rest is a breeze. In fact, my cousin claimed to have dozed off during her procedure. Score one for momma: An extra nap!

Before the procedure began, my aunt put the first round of numbing gel on my lips and we waited twenty minutes while listening to sounds of the rainforest and finding our center, clearing our minds, pondering our existence. My aunt is a child of the 60's but don't tell her I told you that. She likes to think she's in the under-40 category and since she knows how to use a tattoo needle, I'm not about to tell her otherwise.

Finally, my aunt announced that we were ready to begin. The first pass? Easy! I felt very little. I closed my eyes, as my aunt applied the next layer of numbing gel and waiting for the second of six passes. I had just settled in when all of a sudden, my lips were being stung by tiny little hornets that must have come in looking for the source of the nature noises blaring through the surround sound. I opened an eye to make sure I was swatting at the nasty little bugs and not my aunt when I discovered that Hey! It *was* my aunt! And round two was over. Numbing gel generously applied. *Namaste*—I found my center, I said my "oms" and the third pass began.

Weird, not only were my lips bleeding, I'm pretty sure that the needle was penetrating right to my teeth and were those stars I was seeing? My aunt commented that she'd never had anyone bleed quite like me. I believe her exact words were, "Holy macaroni, girl. You are bleeding like a stuck pig!"

When the fourth pass began, I'm pretty sure I lifted my leg up off the table and rammed it into my aunt's ribs. Sorry, but that's what she gets for using a dull, farm-sized needle to inject my lips with color. And what was that sound? Oh. It was me. Screaming. Kinda like a stuck pig.

In the middle of the fifth pass, somehow, I rose from the table, acquired the tattoo gun and was now chasing my aunt around the room before I finally regained my traumatized mind. Honestly, I'm surprised Cheney didn't order lip tattooing instead of waterboarding. I know I was telling my aunt all kinds of secrets. Eventually, though, enough was enough. My aunt said she thought my lips had sufficient color and that if I gave her the tattooing instrument before the police arrived, she wouldn't press charges. She's very generous in that way.

So, my lips were done. I looked in the mirror and couldn't see my face for those big red blobs on the mirror, which looked like smoked ham hocks right above my chin … Oh. Those are my lips. Angelina would have been jealous. Overall, despite the spitting in unknown tongues that the pain caused me, I was very pleased with the outcome. Then my aunt put her arm around me and was nudging me back onto the table.

"Are you ready to do your eyes?" she asked very sweetly while turning up the soothing sounds of whales in heat.

Her nose only bled for a few minutes, and she doesn't flinch anymore when I hug her at our family reunions, so I think we're all good. Best of all, the restraining order's been lifted and I'm allowed to enter the great state of Texas once again.

And? The good news? Not having to apply lipstick in the mornings has clearly shaved one half minute off my morning routine. And that's clearly worth another snooze--if I don't use shampoo in the shower.

Sexy Back

It was a typical Thursday morning—crazy, naturally, but not unusually so. Luckily, my daughters decided to take matters into their own hands. They did their own hair and picked out their own clothes and lied about brushing their teeth without a moment's worth of grumbling. My younger daughter asked to borrow something of mine; I nodded my approval as I tossed a still-frozen strudel at each girl. Breakfast was done and we were out the door.

With only moments to spare, I pulled into their school and slowed the van down as they jumped out the side door. My younger daughter turned to blow me a kiss; her little side ponytail was starting to fall a little bit. She looked cute, nonetheless; I was so proud of her for doing her own hair. It's not every 7-year old that can create her own side ponytail, ya know. That kid was going to go places. My heart got weepy thinking about how much I loved that independent little world-changer.

That afternoon, however, school sent home an entirely different kid.

As she crawled into the van, she cried out, "Momma, your leopard pony tail holder is crap. Absolute CRAP!"

"Excuse me?" I countered hoping that my tone and word choice would indicate that I didn't appreciate such language coming from the mouth of my baby girl, future CEO of some major international, multi-galactic corporation and caregiver of her tired and aged momma.

"You heard me—it's CRAP!" she continued, failing

to notice that her audience (me) was completely lost. "It was hard enough getting it to work right the first time, but then it came out in the middle of reading. So, I had to put my hair back up without a mirror because my teacher wouldn't let me go to the bathroom even though it wasn't my turn to read. Then it came out again when we were going to centers and I asked Robbie to help me, but he was no help. He said he didn't even know how to put in a *regular* ponytail holder. He really couldn't do a complicated ponytail holder like yours. Then my teacher said she'd help me, but she didn't know how to work that ponytail holder either and she made me put it in my backpack. She said I couldn't wear it to school ever again. Thanks, Momma. Thanks for buying a leopard, stupid, no-good ponytail holder that's crap."

Oh for heaven's sake. I had no idea what she was talking about. I didn't even have a leopard ponytail holder. The only leopard print thing I owned was …

Oh geez.

Oh … well, she was right: Oh crap.

I felt all the blood rush to my face, and I felt my heart literally stop beating for just a second or two as I recalled the only leopard thing I owned.

See, there comes a time in every momma's life when mommahood just slaps the sexy right out of ya.

When I've been up way too late cleaning puke and way too early cooking waffles …

When I've sprinkled Parmesan cheese on the hamburger helper for the third night in a row in an attempt to appear gourmet …

When I've skipped my shower because my hair doesn't look horrible and I want that extra fifteen minutes of sleep …

When I've resorted to wearing the holey (and I don't mean close to God) underwear because somehow between 8:00am and 4:00pm, when we were out of the house, someone sprinkled water on the laundry and it multiplied …

When I've dragged my tired tooshie into bed after doing an hour's worth of partial sum-algorithms with a second grader—yes a second grader and no, I still don't get understand how to do them—and my husband reaches over and caresses said-tired tooshie and I hear myself growl at him (and not in a Carmen Electra-type growl) …

That's when I know the sexy's done been slapped right outta my stinky self. I found myself in that situation just three months ago. I stole a few moments to run into the local department store and purchase my first—and only—leopard print item in an effort to bring sexy back. Well, as much as a tired, overworked momma can do such a thing.

It had been worn once … for less than five minutes (time is of the essence when you're a momma). Afterwards, it wad been socked away in the sock drawer for all time (or at least until I felt frisky again) … hidden away from any little pilfering hands. Until that morning, apparently, when it had been found and repurposed.

Oh crap indeed, baby girl. I drove on through the pick-up lane. I'd have sped if the Prius-momma ahead of me would have just used her accelerator.

I saw my innocent baby girl's teacher smile and wave really big as I drove by.

I. Was. Mortified.

From the back seat, my frustrated daughter pulled my

leopard-print ***thong*** from her backpack and threw it into the front seat. "Here!" she huffed. "I will never wear that again!"

A momma can only hope, baby girl. A momma can only hope.

Brunette Sunset #632 Looks Good On Everyone

My hair has recently been colored and I have been promised shiny, healthy, grey-free hair for the next six to eight weeks. In my life, that should roughly equate six to eight days.

I just turned 40, but in momma years, I'm about 82 years old, and I have a head full of grey hair. I discovered my very first touch of frost when I was 20 years old, after the Sun-In orange had grown out and my hair was somewhat my natural brunette color. I was at the mall buying NKOTB's posters and Richard Marx's cassettes when my friend pointed out my grey. I freaked! I was 20 and that's what 20-year-olds do—they freak. I did it very well. I was a master freaker. We raced to Hellmart before it closed (those were the days when the day actually ended) and bought my first official, non-spray-in color.

I have since run the gamut—highlighting, frosting, dying, lowlighting, plucking the tiny strands of white right out. I have done it all. And I'll tell ya—I have finally reached a point in my life where it's just not worth it anymore.

I could easily tell you that the grey defines me: This (pointing to the grey at my left temple) is the grey I got when I hit a deer driving to work in my brand new Chevy Cavalier—the very first car I ever owned and the very first stick shift I ever drove. This (pointing to the grey in the middle of my widow's peak) is the grey I got when we went through fertility treatments to have Daughter 1 and then Daughter 2. This (pointing to the grey at the crown of my head) is the grey I got when Brian spent a week in the hospital with pneumonia. This (pointing to the grey behind my ear) is the grey I got when I lost my own dad. This (pointing to the grey at the nape of my neck) is the grey I got when I earned my Masters degree.

But owning my grey is sappy and I'm not sappy until I have had my two glasses of sangria and my Aunt Flo is visiting.

Besides, that is not at all why I have decided to no longer wash that grey right outta my hair. Nope. The reason I'm no longer gonna mask my premature grey-ish hair is that I'm way too lazy and way too cheap.

See, if I pay someone to color my hair, I also have to pay someone to watch The Daughters. And when I get back home, there will have been some sort of catastrophe that will have cost me combat pay for the sitter and the dye job will only last three weeks, tops.

And if I color my hair at home, I'll have to wait until The Daughters are in bed because they will cause me to color the carpet and the tile and the walls as I'd have to run around slinging dye all over the house chasing them down because they will have let the dog in the house and the dog will have eaten the dinner I had set out. I speak from experience … the walls look kind of marbled now, though, so it's all good.

I would also have to wait until The Daughters were in bed, otherwise they would know I colored my hair and the next thing you know, they would have the microphone at church, announcing during Joys and Concerns that their momma has grey hair.

But the real reason I can't dye my hair after they go to bed is that is the time I dig out the mint chocolate chip ice cream and watch reruns of *Friends*, pretending to be Rachel-who does *not* have grey hair.

And quite frankly, I'm not ready to give up my ice cream (or, heaven forbid, share it!) And I am certainly not ready to give up my late-night *Friends* just so that I can have young-looking, not-grey hair.

Therefore, Mother Nature, I'm allowing you to do your thing: Frost my hair because I'm not messing with it anymore. At least not this week.

But next week, when a "well-meaning" acquaintance at Hellmart declares, "Oh, I didn't know you were getting grey," I will, once again, let Lady Clairol into my home. But only after I've had my ice cream.

Exercise Will Kill Me

The wise sage who said that exercise relieves stress has obviously never walked a mile in my body. I try to exercise; honestly, I do. It just doesn't work out for me. Ever.

Brian is a morning person *and* an exerciser. This means that he's up at the crack of dawn and ready to go, do, sweat, burn calories. I, on the other hand, believe that all the world's problems would go away if we were allowed to sleep until after ten.

When Brian and I were first married, he wanted me to get up and exercise with him. Because I was a loving and naïve wife, I decided that I should do whatever he asked of me. We were newlyweds. I have no idea what I was thinking; the ring was on my finger already!

One summer morning, he woke me up and I somehow managed to get dressed and we set out to walk. By the time we got to the end (of the sidewalk), I was in tears, begging to go back home … to bed … to my pillow! "Honey," my beloved new husband gently said as he took my arm and helped me up from the bush where I had heaped my body and now lay sobbing, "We're not even out of our yard yet."

As a compromise, we decided to meet after work at the local YMCA, where there exists a running track around their basketball court. Brian could play basketball and I could walk around the track. As mentioned before, I try to exercise—hell, sometimes I even WANT to exercise—my body, on the other hand? It rebels. On this particular venture, I decided I wanted to run. To be clear: I have never been a runner. On field day in junior high, I was always on the tug-of-war team or I threw the shot put. I was never in the *track* part of the track-and-field sports. But, I decided to run anyway. I made one lap around the track when a baller hollered up to me, "Lady? You okay?" Okay? Is he talking to me? I'm just running. I look around. No one else is on the track. I holler back, "Me?" And my sweetheart cries out, "Yes, you, lady! You having a seizure? (snicker, snicker)"

Thus my running career started and ended.

Thus Brian's sleeping-on-the-couch career started.

Once our sweet babies came along, we would go out as a family, strollers filled with our baby girls. We'd casually walk around the neighborhood and call it exercise. Then the daughters became independent and wanted to walk on their own. We'd casually walk around half the neighborhood and then limp around the other half carrying our not-so-independent daughters back home.

To this end, we invested in bikes. I hadn't ridden a bike in twenty years. But, you know what they say about riding a bike: You'd better have pretty good insurance.

Brian's bike, of course, was custom built. It had every bell and whistle on it that bikes could have, including, well, bells and whistles. Daughter 1 had her shiny pink bike with streamers. Daughter 2 had her own little trailer on the back of Brian's bike (told ya—it had *everything*). I had a bike that we were assured would be simple to use. Start and go. Easy peasy.

Unfortunately, I could only remember how to go fast. I took off down the sloped driveway and into the street and couldn't stop myself. I remember hearing Daughter 1 holler, "Wait up, Momma!" I heard Brian saying, "Show off." What they couldn't hear was me whimpering because I couldn't remember exactly how to stop the thing or slow down without throwing myself into the path of my own forward-moving bike!

Always the competitor, Brian eventually caught up to me. I was crying, "I don't remember how to stop!"

"Use the breaks," The ever-so-useful-advice-giving Dad said.

"How?" I moaned, feeling very much like a passenger on the bus in *Speed.* I was certain I was doing about sixty.

"Squeeze 'em," Brian said. So, I squeezed 'em. And then I flipped over the handlebars. My bike helmet was twisted around my head so that I looked like a hockey goalie. My knees were bleeding, my elbows were swollen and curse words were escaping my mouth heading straight toward the daughters' ears.

The bikes? Not such a great exercise tool.

Eventually, I was able to be around bikes again. But our family's choice of exercise became Daughter 1, Daughter 2 and Brian on the death contraptions with me walking beside them. I realized, quickly, about six blocks from home, that this was a convenient and effective method of exercising. The first six blocks were my warm up so that the last six blocks, I could carry Daughter 2 (and her bike) back home because she would get "tiredy."

While an efficient means of exercise—and quite a cardio workout— hauling a 3-year-old on your hunched-over back, dragging the Little Mermaid bicycle six blocks is not an ideal situation and certainly not as much of a stress reliever as one would think it would be.

Brian suggested that maybe outdoors wasn't my cup of tea. Maybe I exercised best when I stuck the kids in the gym's nursery and worked out on a machine programmed to do its job … there's no way to mess that up, right? Personally, I thought I exercised best when I stuck the kids in the gym's nursery and hit the mall for a pedicure, but we don't all see the world in the same way, do we?

Ever wanting to please my husband (snort), I tried it his way. Besides that, the gym said I couldn't go to the mall and the pedicurist said he wouldn't come to the gym. So much for compromising on *their* parts.

After dropping the daughters off and leaving a fake cell number, I was introduced to a medieval torture device that I'm sure I saw in that scene from *Braveheart,* where Mel Gibson shouts out, "9-1-1!" right before he leaves his beloved Scotland for the last time. The trainer called it an "elliptical machine." That's just semantics as far as I'm concerned. "Torture device" is just not as easy to sell.

I did about five hours on that thing. The trainer said it was only three minutes, but he was young and stupid and his digital watch was upside down on his wrist. I finished my time and fell off the machine onto a treadmill, knocking a woman off the back and found myself hunched over a stationary bike, which became not so stationary about the time I landed on it and drove it into one of those ever-so-flattering mirrors in the gym. Feeling very much like William Wallace there toward the end, I hollered out, "Freedom!" grabbed the daughters and have never been back to that gym again.

I'd try a Zumba class, but I'm afraid I'd have to have my legs surgically untied from each other after the first ten minutes.

Tales Of Carmen Electra And Me

Despite what my body looks like, I haven't completely given up on exercise. Eventually, I found myself working with my best friends, and we decided that we'd work together after hours to become healthy and vibrant women. We yoga'd. We walked. We danced. And I found myself enjoying exercise. Wait. That's not right. Enjoying is too strong of a word: I found myself exercising despite myself so I could get the good gossip from my besties.

My workout peeps and I wanted to change up our routine a little. Really, we didn't *want* to change up anything, but we came across a workout DVD that we just couldn't pass up: Carmen Electra's *Aerobic Striptease*.

It does so exist. Google it. It's a real workout.

The first time we did the workout (yes, it really is a real workout!), we giggled through half of it. We giggled partially because we were learning (and botching) stripper moves and partially because, deep in our souls, we're still 13 years old.

We also giggled because Carmen told us to "never underestimate the power of a finger in your mouth." Really. She told us that. And? According to Brian (and all the other husbands in our group) there really is power in that one little move. Try it. Go ahead; mark your place because the significant other in your life won't let you return to reading after he sees the finger in your mouth.

You're back. So soon? (Don't tell your honey I said that.)

Despite what notions Carmen conjures in your minds, it really was a good workout. So much so that we Carmen-wannabes met together over our winter break and continued the workout. Then we had yet another unexpected break due to the sixty-three inches of snow on the ground. Because I'm a great leader (or an antagonist), I texted my girls: Do the Carmen workout … at home … for our husbands.

I don't know how many male readers I have, but I can hear them all say, in their best Austin Powers voices, "Yeah, Baby!"

Or maybe I'm still hearing an echo of Brian saying that.

I can't report on my tight-spandex-wearing friends and their adventures, but I can tell you about mine.

Don't worry, Mom and Mom-in-law, I'll keep it family friendly.

First off, when I do this routine with my Carmen Cronies, I am wearing torn sweats and tube socks and my hair's pulled back in a scrunchie. No, they didn't stop making them in 1989, although my scrunchie actually is from 1989. This ensemble doesn't work for an at-home aerobic display with a one-very-happy-man audience. In trying to come up with fun stage attire, I realized two things about my wardrobe: 1. My clothes accurately reflect who I am (a harried, minivan-driving momma); and 2. I don't own any panties that could be considered—in any way, shape or form—pretty, lovely, sexy or otherwise attractive. Even my own grandma would approve of every single pair of my panties.

Secondly, I didn't realize just how bright the lights are in our house. I spent probably five minutes turning out lights all through the house. It's not that I was embarrassed by this whole ordeal. I was setting the tone, the mood—contributing to the ambiance of the routine by making our house look like a strip club … or at least what I have been *told* a strip club looks like.

Ahem. Where was I?

Having been warned by one of my besties that Radio Disney and Kidz Bop don't have any good music selections for our challenge, I spent an evening downloading songs that were confirmed by Google itself to be "hot stripping songs." So, I put on the music and was so intent on trying to remember the routine that I was shocked by the lyrics. Really? Did I just pay good money to download a song that says stuff like *that*? Then I vocalized this concern to Brian who said that he didn't care what I or the song was saying as long as I kept the workout up. He's so concerned for my physical well-being.

And the giggling? It came back. And apparently, giggling for the first ten minutes of the dance was not quite what Brian was expecting. I'm not sure how Carmen feels about giggling either. However, I did look it up and that ten minutes of giggling and shaking my head and blushing burned about 130 calories. So there.

I finally got the giggling under control and attempted to actually remove some of my clothing in a motion that I made up all by myself. Then I accidently began to strangle myself performing this movement. Eventually, I had to stop my super-hot moves and let Brian help me get this particular article of clothing untangled from my hair. I'm sure I could have done it on my own, but it was covering my eyes and I accidently bumped into the corner and made myself dizzy.

Halfway through the routine—okay, fine, five minutes into the routine—I needed a drink. It's important to keep up the hydration. Plus, the giggling had started again, so it seemed like a good time to take a break. This was not part of what Brian was expecting, but he went and got me a drink anyway. Hell! He brought me three drinks: a glass of white wine, a glass of sangria and orange juice that had a great kick to it. What a guy!

By this point, however, I was not even sure where in the routine I was and started over. Finally, I remembered the immortal words of Carmen, my workout muse: Always transition from one move to another by slapping your butt. Or something like that. So, I slapped. And *Bam*! It happened.

Daughter 2 burst into our room, used our bathroom and reported that she had a bad dream.

That never happens in Carmen's routine.

After I carried Daughter 2 back to bed and assured her that dinosaurs are no longer roaming the earth nor are they trampling through Momma and Daddy's bedroom, I walked in, ready to start my routine again.

By this time, however, I was cold and my audience was not as enthusiastic as he had been twenty minutes earlier. So, I channeled Carmen, and I used the power of a finger in my mouth.

And, as the old saying goes, the fat lady sang! [Note from my Editor: *I can't believe you just wrote that.*] [Note from me: *Believe it, baby. Just wait until the second book.*]

5Ks are for Wussies. I Am Queen of the Wussies.

A few months back, my workout peeps and I decided to do a 5K. Then the day of the 5K came and we decided, since we hadn't trained at all, we wouldn't do that particular 5K.

Good news, though! There's always a 5K somewhere. We decided we would do a 5K ... and we'd train for it ... and it would be a good time. Looking back, I'm not sure that any of us really knew a precise definition of "good time."

The weekend of the 5K came and went. I found myself in the recliner with ice on every single joint on my body. I also chewed ibuprofen like candy. The carnage went down like this:

There were five of us who worked out together. Two of us (and our husbands) actually completed the 5K. The others apparently felt that work deadlines, sick kids and family dinners took precedent over completing a 5K with their friends. Obviously, they don't have the same ethics as my lone 5K friend, FloJo, and I have.

When we registered on race day, Brian and I opted to not get the time chip for our shoes. "Oh no!" my overly enthusiastic FloJo exclaimed, "You need to keep your time!" So, Brian and I got chipped and it was time to go.

I had no idea what keeping time would mean. An hour later, I learned that the time I earned would be used by the woman who finished directly in front of me when she said, "At least it didn't take me, ummm ..." finger scrolling down the printed times to my name, "forty-five minutes to finish this race."

Before the race even started, I realized that I was positioned completely wrong. I was front and center. This, my friends, would have led to me getting completely trampled by the die-hard runners, including my friend FloJo. So, I moved to the back of the pack and began my preparations.

Some people were stretching. Some people were running the block warming up. I was trying to figure out how to get Daughter 1's MP3 player to play my much-thought-out 5K playlist. Finally, the Black Eyed Peas began telling me that tonight was going to be a good, good night, and I was ready. Unfortunately, I was now at the very, very back of the pack as the gun had sounded and everyone else had taken off. I was standing alone in the street with my earphones drowning out the shouts of, "Run, stupid!"

I shot from my spot and ran! It felt glorious! I was *running*! My feet pounded the pavement. My arms pumped in time. My ears rang with the sounds of the MP3 *and* my pulse as it kept time with Will.i.am. It was probably at this point that I realized the shelf-bra in my tank top was not the same as sports bra. Not that I needed a *lot* of support, but I was amazingly surprised that my jiggling was actually tapping my chin. Who knew my not-remotely-perky B cups were stretchy? I'm pretty sure by the time I finished the race I had gained three inches of length in my boobs.

While I started off like a sled dog mushing through the Iditarod, I eventually reached a point when I didn't think I could take one more step; I turned the corner. I had run the first block. I'll say that again: I had run just the first block. Obviously, I was going to have to pace myself.

Having never been in a real live organized run before (*except for sixth grade, when I was in a relay, and I remember nothing of it because when I tossed off my baton, I saw my friend from Girl Scouts, so we stood and chatted while the other racers whizzed right by us*), I wondered how the race officials would keep us safe from traffic. Quickly, I learned that a couple of security personnel would bring up the tail of the race in a four-wheeler. I know this because these guys rode my tail the *entire* time. I'm pretty sure I heard one of them say, "Pick up the pace, Granny" but I was afraid to turn around. They were packin' heat.

While I appreciated this security, and I appreciated the fact that they kept traffic from interrupting our pace by keeping the side streets blocked, this made it very difficult—nay, impossible—for me to cut off on a side street and shave a few miles off my journey. Well, played, overweight glorified mall cops, well played.

As my pace continued, so did my playlist and I soon learned that I couldn't multitask. As much as I grew to despise the additional security who kept me on the actual track, they were friendly and encouraging. As I passed each intersection, they would cheer, "Good for you!" or "Keep it up!" I, in turn, who can't apparently run and listen to music at the same time, would sing the line from my current MP3 song. This resulted in my saying such things as, "Let's Get Physical!" and "It's the Thrill of the Fight!" and "Save a Horse, Ride a Cowboy!" and, my favorite, thanks to Meredith Brooks, "I'm a Bitch." Nice.

At the halfway point, I totally felt like a runner as I ~~accepted took~~ snatched a glass of water from a volunteer who held it out to me at the turning point. I gulped the water, spilling half of it down my front, and then I proceeded to choke. And cough. And hack. The volunteer came out and whacked me on the back. Even the four-wheeler coppers asked if I was okay. It might have been the highlight of my run.

I was all right and eventually stopped coughing, so I continued on.

About a half mile from the finish line, FloJo jogged back to finish the race with me.

"Oh, man!" She breathlessly exclaimed, with nary a drop of sweat on her brow, "I couldn't run the whole thing! I had to take several breaks and walk a lot!"

Whew, so I wasn't alone. Even though I didn't walk "a lot." I walked the whole damned thing. I was a tad bit relieved that even my much-better-trained friend, FloJo, who did own a real-live sports bra (and knew how to wear it), didn't fair very well on our first 5K together. According to her.

As FloJo and I crossed the finish line together—tight like spandex were we!—Brian and FloJo's husband approached us with the news: FloJo had finished third in our age division (which is the colored hair to grey hair category). I, in contrast, finished dead last … in all age divisions.

As she accepted her trophy, FloJo posed for the cameras. Okay, there was just one camera, but she worked it like it was a street corner on Sunset Boulevard. I posed for the official race nurse who handed me a handful of ibuprofen and a bottle of water. Truth? I preferred the over-the-counter relief to the trophy. Besides, I can steal it from FloJo's mantle next time I visit.

Actual* Conversation with a Personal Trainer

Trainer: Ok, what's your favorite exercise?

Me: I don't understand your question.

Trainer: What do you like to do for exercise?

Me: Sorry. Still not getting what you're asking.

Trainer: Do you like to do Zumba, strength training, stretching?

Me: Sorry, but I only speak English. [*speaking extra loud and extra slow*] Dude, I don't get those words.

Trainer: What's your favorite physical activity?

Me: My favorite thing to do is lay on the couch and read. After that, it's pretty much a crapshoot as to what I like to do.

Trainer: Well, then, why don't we just hop on the treadmill?

Me: Bad knee. Doctor said no hopping.

Trainer: I don't think you're taking your workout program seriously.

Me: Look at me! (dusting off powdered sugar from my increasingly-floppy chest) I think you are correct, sir!

Trainer: Tell me what you hope to get out of our program.

Me: Yes, I hope to get out of the program.

Trainer: No. What's your goal? What are you hoping for?

Me: A miracle. Unless that's too much effort.

*The word "actual" in this particular case is defined as the silly dialogue that runs through my head as I'm forced to do twelve—yes, twelve—push ups in the middle of a stinky gym with a size negative two trainer (whose thighs don't even recognize each other because they've never met each other) standing over me telling me I was "almost there." Know what? I didn't know where I was going and I sure as hell didn't ever feel like I had arrived.

Holey Underwear: A Story Not About God

Even though Brian oft times has very little regard for my plight as a busy, tired Momma, he does, when it counts, hold me in high esteem. As Tammy Wynette says, "After all, he's just a man" and he does the best he can. Regardless of what his actions convey, he does always have me at the forefront of his thoughts. Usually I'm wearing the cute little lacy red thing. But whatever works, right?

When it comes to special occasions, our conversation is the same regardless of the event: Birthday, Christmas, Anniversary and-in this particular case-Mother's Day.

Brian: What do you want for (fill-in-the-blank with the name of upcoming holiday)?

Me: Oh. I don't know… whatever you want to get me. Surprise me.

Brian: Great!!! I look forward to surprising you!

No, wait; that's not at all what Brian says. He says something along the lines of this, "Great. Surprise you? No way. Why can't you just say what you want? If I had an idea of what to give you, I wouldn't have asked in the first place." And actually, he mutters this. He doesn't think I can hear him, but I can. I can always hear him mumbling thanks to that one Christmas where he surprised me with the "TV Ears" (As seen on TV! Only

$19.95!). The gift that comes back to bite the giver in the butt.

Honestly, I'm not sure why I'm not more direct and don't just ask him for something that I really, really want. I'm not sure why I feel it necessary to ask him to surprise me other than I know that it causes him great squirminess and I kinda like to see him squirm! And I don't want to be the only one in the house that's a thinker.

In the past, I've gotten all kinds of interesting "surprises": the Christmas ornament that I thought The Daughters made (but really, Brian had made it); the umbrella that he got from a vendor at work (the third of its kind); and the certificate entitling me to three nights worth of "anything my heart desired" in a "bedroom of my choice"—I chose a bedroom at the Holiday Inn Express watching 80s chick flicks starring Meg Ryan and sleeping in. I have yet to receive another of those coupons. Dammit.

This year, however, was different. It seemed that after almost thirteen years as a couple, Brian finally got me: He gave me a laundry-free weekend and a dinner where I didn't have to share, cut or clean anything for me or anyone else plus a Sunday afternoon nap without interruption from anyone under the age of 39. Momma heaven. I love this man. Please … give me a moment to compose myself.

[gulp]

Mother's Day weekend started off great. I met a friend and scrapbooked until well past our bedtime then I ran to Hellmart and got groceries at 12:38 in the morning without kids. I wanted to make sure that Saturday and Sunday were as completely free as possible.

(By the way, there are certain advantages to shopping Hellmart at that particular time. For starters, The Daughters are home and in bed, so it's easier for me to stick to my list and not buy things like strawberry milk (that they're sure they'll like now even though they've never liked it before), brightly colored fish-shaped crackers and fudge-dipped, mint-flavored Oreos. Okay—I did buy the fudge-dipped, mint-flavored Oreos. The advantage was that I got to hide them without anyone else even knew there were in the house. Score one for Momma.

However, there are certain disadvantages as well. For starters, I didn't get any" free examples," as The Daughters excitedly call them, of yogurt or pizza rolls; there are all kinds of crazies in Hellmart at the time of night; and apparently, there will be only one working register for every thirteen shoppers ready to check out. Obviously, that rule came down from corporate and is apparently a 24-hour rule.)

Where was I? Oh yeah. Mother's Day

Saturday morning, Brian got started on laundry then left for the day with explicit instructions that I was not to do laundry.

I told him in no uncertain terms that he did not have to tell me twice. The laundry was his for the weekend.

Saturday evening, when Brian returned, we dropped The Daughters off with their Nana. It was Mother's Day weekend, of course, and she really did want to spend two or three hours with some wound-up, vampire-playing girls. (You're welcome, Nana!) Then, Brian and I enjoyed our dinner out, where I willingly (because I wanted to) shared one of my freshly made, Cajun-spiced kettle chips with Brian, but other than that, it was all mine.

[Imagine evil "Bwahahaha" laugh here.]

Sunday afternoon, after a wonderful lunch and a great visit with family, I got to enjoy my two-hour nap while Brian and The Daughters hung out by the pool (in fifty degree weather).

Overall, it was certainly a great weekend. Brian's idea was right on target. I couldn't have asked for anything better for Mother's Day! I couldn't have imagined a better surprise from my guy on my special day!

… except that when Sunday night arrived, Brian was still doing laundry.

And, of course, my underwear was, at bedtime, being sorted into the laundry holding pattern.

That, of course, meant that I would obviously have to do one of two things: 1. Wear the holey underwear that every momma has stashed in the back of her undie drawer, just in case; or 2. Go commando.

So, my friends, I'd like to issue a public apology if you saw me that special week in May. I'd like to apologize in advance for either scratching through my holes or fidgeting in my commando-ness. Either way, it surely was not pretty. But, what can I say? I was ordered to not touch the laundry and I pledged to love, honor and obey when I married my macho man. Not really on the "obey" part—I snorted during that particular word when the Justice of the Peace requested that I "say what I say." I'd like to acknowledge that the omission was calculated and the snort through the word was my own personal way of saying, "We've come a long way, Baby!" But, the truth of the matter is this: The week before we eloped,

Brian offered to do the laundry … and well, I was commando on my wedding day and totally distracted.

Actual* Conversation with Daughter 2 in the Laundry Room

Daughter 2: Momma, I think I left something in my pocket. Did you find it in the laundry?

Me: What did you leave?

Daughter 2: Ummmmmm… [looking at the dryer as I'm unloading]

Me: [arms crossed over my chest realizing that I'll never get anything accomplished with this train of through steaming through the laundry room; I bend down to the dryer] Okay. Here's a rock. Was it this rock?

Daughter 2: No. But that is my rock. Thanks. I have missed this rock since I was a little girl.

Me: That long, huh? Here's a dime and a quarter.

Daughter 2: Oh! That's mine. I was going to buy ice cream. But this isn't what I lost.

Me: I just found a bookmark-is this yours?

Daughter 2: Yeah, but I don't want it anymore. You can have it.

Me: Thanks. Here's a seashell.

Daughter 2: Ahhhhh … I love this seashell. Yeah, it's mine. But don't tell Daughter 1 that I have it, promise?

Me: Promise. Honey … what are you looking for?

Daughter 2: Ummm [scratches her little head and then taps her little foot]… what was it? Oh yeah! My frog? Is my frog in there?

*The word "actual" in this particular case is completely and totally true. Send chocolate and sympathy cards.

Richard Marx Knew Nothing About Endless Summer Nights

During the first few years of momma-hood, I dreamed that I would have wonderful summers where The Daughters and I would grow our own watermelons and then make pickles out of the leftover rind. I'm sure we wouldn't eat that crap, of course. We'd learn to sew our own clothes and knit our fall sweaters and scarves. We'd have karaoke contests. We'd tie-dye shirts and shorts and sheets. We'd cook out every night trying new recipes for Brian, who probably also wouldn't eat that crap—he's picky that way. We'd take all kinds of road trips and find fun places to go swimming and touring and shopping and playing. We'd redesign our home and paint and make new pillows to give a dull room a brand-new look. We'd read great books and then act them out and make our own videos. We'd discover new sports and play them in our back yard. We'd swim! We'd bike! We'd live life to the fullest! We'd be a friggin' Norman Rockwell painting.

Let me tell you what, it happened. All of that happened. When The Daughters had their first school summer vacation, we did all of those things. In the first week. Then, we were "bored" and there was "nothing to do." But, I learned ... Oh, how I learned.

The next year, I began in January, calling every church in town and scheduled a morning and evening Vacation Bible School for each week of the summer. I didn't care if the church had live snakes ready for those called to handle them, my kids were signed up and going. Then, in the in-between time, I signed up for every other camp I could find: gymnastics, art, weaving, beauty, softball, soccer, music, swimming (it was really swimming lessons, but The Daughters bought into the camp concept much more quickly than "lessons"). The Daughters did it all. And I would faithfully load up the minivan and MapQuest the best route to take when I picked them up from VBS in order to get Daughter 1 to play-dough camp and Daughter 2 to trampoline camp without either one being late. Every once in a while, we'd be stuck at home and have to do "laundry camp" and "cleaning the toilet camp;" these usually won out to "Disney Channel camp." Hey! No one can expect me to be full of educational opportunities twelve months out of the year without some serious cranberry-vodka popcicles coming into play.

One particular summer day when we had no camps scheduled and it wasn't raining and I had temporarily lost my mind, I told The Daughters I'd take them to our local water park. I told them we'd go right after breakfast. As soon as the strudels were thawed, we loaded up the minivan and headed to Splashaway Island.

We got as far as the corner when Daughter 1 asked me if I had grabbed her swimsuit. I was wearing my suit; Daughter 2 was wearing her suit. Daughter 1 had left her suit hanging on the back of the bathroom door. We turned around.

Again, we pulled out of the driveway and turned the corner, Daughter 2 asked if Splashaway Island had towels. I pulled into the next driveway and headed back toward home to retrieve towels that wouldn't be provided by the water park.

For the third time, we pulled out of the driveway, turned the corner and got to the stoplight when Daughter 1 decided she would put on her sunscreen in the minivan to save time once we got to the waterpark. Good idea! I encouraged her and her sister to do just that. The only problem with this was that we didn't have the sunscreen. I did a U-turn and returned home.

Three more times we left the house and returned. Daughter 2 didn't have her flip-flops on. Daughter 1 and Daughter 2 both had to go to the bathroom, "And not just to pee." And then there was the little matter of a licensed driver actually being in possession of her license.

I was utterly and completely exhausted by the time we arrived at Splashaway Island. I almost fell asleep sitting in my lounger beside the wave pool. I say almost because I'm not sure what the statue of limitations is on child-neglect-at-a-water-park and I know that everything I write can and will be used against me.

Next summer, I won't be so lazy as to leave a day unscheduled. Momma needs her rest.

Conspiracy Theories: You Can't Trust Them

When I was pregnant with Daughter 1, I read all the books and researched all the latest parenting theories (all of which can basically be summed up with three little words: Don't Screw Up). And like most new moms, I completely forgot everything I read when I had my very first contraction.

With Daughter 2, I watched a Dr. "Feel" show (as Daughter 1 used to call him) about Attachment Parenting. Attachment Parenting embraces (literally) the philosophy that the child is never without the touch of a parent at all times during the first few months or so of his/her precious little life.

*Note to all readers: I know there's more to it … please don't start the hate mail before the fan mail really takes off.

The guest on Dr. Feel had a 29-month old that she was practicing attachment parenting with. And I say practicing because the kid was 2 ½! That meant that he was all. Over. The. Place. His worn, wrinkled and quickly-greying-before-the-live-studio-audience's-eyes momma was doing her damnedest to keep up with her little A.D.D. poster child. My first thought was that it's never too young to discuss Ritalin with your pediatrician. (*Again — do not start the hate mail!) Then, briefly, I thought I might like to try Attachment Parenting with Daughter 2.

Briefly.

Several knocks on reality's door brought me out of that little fantasy. For starters, I work full-time outside the home, and I couldn't take my baby with me to teach Romeo and Juliet to 140 high school freshmen. Secondly, I was already tired of her touching my bladder with her tiny little feet from the inside, and I didn't have a choice in that touch. Once she was out, I didn't have to put up with it 24/7 anymore. And then finally, I had a contraction and completely forgot what I was even thinking. I just had a leg cramp and forgot what I was writing.

Oh yeah. Attachment Parenting.

The good news is that Daughter 2 is now 5 years old and is perfectly healthy and well adjusted (despite what her kindergarten teacher has hinted at during parent teacher conferences). The not-so-good news is that she practices, against my will, her own version of Attachment Parenting: I call it Attachment Sleeping. This is a new "parenting" theory. And if she is able to sell it, I'm totally cashing in on my kid's good fortune. See, in her approach to raising her parents, she's decided that she must, at all times during the sleeping hours, be touching her momma. Lucky me. Dammit.

Until she makes money with this craziness, however, I'm going to be one cranky momma.

Let me tell you about our bed-situation, first. I'm not trying to brag about what will sound like a very huge assortment of sleeping apparatuses, but I'm just stating the facts: Brian and I share a king-sized bed. Daughter 1 has two daybeds in her room. Daughter 2 has a full-sized bed in her room. We have two couches, two love seats and a recliner. If—and let me re-emphasize that—If we needed to, we could put a kid in bed with us and then fit nine other (relatively small) people in our home to sleep. Not that I ever want to try that. Who would cook them breakfast? Sure wouldn't be me.

So, our bedtime routine is this: We put the Daughters in their beds about 8:00. We turn the lights out at 8:15. We scream at them to settle down and go to sleep until 9:00 and then finally … usually … they go sleep around 9:30 if all is right in the world. It's never all right in the world.

Brian and I want to be in our bed asleep between 10:30 and 11:00. However, we are usually asleep in the recliner and on the couch about 10:00. Screaming wears a parent out, yo.

Somewhere around 11:15 is when Daughter 2 begins her regime of Attachment Sleeping. She'll crawl in bed with Brian and me, gently pat Brian's face, and then plant herself firmly on my neck. I will push her off; I will elbow her over; I will carry her back to her own bed and she somehow will beat me back to my own bed. So, I'll eventually give up and go sleep in her bed.

Her bed? It will be wet. This never fails. She'll have on "night-time panties" and still manage to pee her bed. So, I'll strip her bed and go crawl into Daughter 1's extra bed. I'll just get settled in and discover that somehow Daughter 2 is now in bed-in the small, single-sleeper day bed in Daughter 1's room—with me.

I will leave her—again—and make my way back to my own bed, where I find that Brian has taken his half of the bed out of the top half of our mattress. So, I head into the recliner.

By now, it's 4:00, and I have gotten no sleep. I will decide to turn on the TV and see what's happened in the world since I have (not) been asleep. The minute I snap the TV on, Daughter 2 will appear at my side in the recliner. She'll be whining, and she will mumble that she can't sleep. Then she will ask if she can "just way wif me, pwease?"

I will look at this beautiful baby and all those Attachment Parenting warm fuzzies that I felt from the Dr. Feel show will come rushing back and I'll say to her, "You can lay with me, Baby Girl …" Immediately, she will crawl up to my head and plant her left foot in my appendix and her right foot on my boob and begin drooling in my ear.

Every night.

Every. Single. Night.

Eventually, I'll ease her off of me just in time to hear Brian's alarm going off. I harbor no ill feelings of his full-night's rest as I yank his warm body off the bed by his chest hairs.

Honestly, I thought once I got married, this bed hoppin' would end.

Anatomy Of Momma's Nervous Breakdown

Bedtime at our house is 10:17. Wait. Before calling human services over the late hour, let me take you through a sample night … let's say it's last night, for example.

7:00 Tell The Daughters to brush their teeth. Fight for fifteen minutes about whether or not they actually did brush their teeth, whether or not they picked out the toothpaste that they may or may not like, whether or not they have to floss every single tooth and whether or not they brushed them through the entire ABC song or the fast-forward version. Remind them to wash their faces … then sigh and give up. The dirt will rub off on their pillows, right?

7:15 Tell The Daughters to put on their pajamas. Confirm that they do indeed have clean pjs. Show them the pjs in their drawers and on their floors and under their beds. Remind them that they wore them just last week and they are not too small. Consent to let them wear one of their daddy's T-shirts if they will just put on anything that can be worn to bed.

7:25 Read a chapter out of their favorite books. Reread part of the previous chapter because they cunningly convince me, yet again, that we didn't read that chapter only to say at the end of the previous chapter, "Oh yeah, I remember now, Momma." Then, we'll read an extra chapter because quite frankly I need to know if Percy really did fulfill the prophecy … and I read the book myself six months ago.

7:45 Say our prayers. Argue about the order in which we bless people. Bless them twice and sometimes three times to do it in every conceivable order possible. Discuss Daughter 1's request to not bless a certain boy in her class who (and I quote) "annoys the living pee" out of her, despite telling him three thousand times in a very sweet and polite voice to "Just knock it the heck off!" I then attempt to discuss how everyone, even annoying, stinky boys, need blessing. Argument ensues. Finally, I concede that we can ask that Pee-Annoying Boy not receive any special blessing. Secretly pray for forgiveness. Don't tell Daughter 1. She'd think I was weak.

8:00 Take drinks of water to The Daughters.

8:03 Take cold drinks of water to The Daughters.

8:05 Take colder drinks of water to The Daughters.

8:07 Ignore The Daughter's pleas for cold drinks of water.

8:08 Realize that I never was very good at ignoring and leave drinks of water in the bedrooms despite knowing that this will mean, in more ways than one, a wet bed—or two.

8:10 Finally. Silence. Followed by giggling.

8:11 Investigate the source of giggling: Daughter 1 and Daughter 2 who met up in the bathroom (because of all the cold drinks requested) and are now attempting to pee standing up—just like Brian.

8:13 Change pj's that have now been tinkled on and tuck The Daughters back into bed. Decline, in no uncertain terms, Daughter 1's plea for goodnight prayers

… again. (That kid will win every philosophical argument she gets into) Mop up bathroom floor.

8:25 Jump completely off the couch in response to Daughter 2's blood-chilling scream. Race in to discover that her bed is wet … and her cup is empty. Pull off PJs, pull off sheets. Drag sleeping bag out of closet and throw a naked Daughter 2 back into bed.

8:30 Turn off hall light.

8:35 Turn off hall light.

8:40 Turn off hall light.

8:45 Turn off hall light then hide just beside the hallway entry. Crouch and lay in wait to catch the little lightening bug as she sneaks out of the hallway.

8:50 Get a cramp in my leg and holler for Brian to come and help me get up and walk it out. Walk through the living room and dining room only to discover the light back on. Listen to The Daughter's giggling. Enlist the help of Brian to unscrew the light bulb in the hallway.

9:05 Assure Daughter 2 that the noise she is hearing in her closet is just a cricket.

9:07 Yes. It is just a cricket.

9:09 Promise and pinky swear that the noise is just a cricket.

9:10 Ask Daughter 1 to repeat the story she just told me about Daughter 2 bringing two frogs into the house from the pool and the frogs, which were in the shoe box on the dresser, are now missing. Empty out Daughter 2's closet and find three frogs. Not two. Three. Ask Brian politely to place the frogs back outside in their proper home. Wait. Did I say, "Ask?" What I meant to say was told. Wait. Not told. Commanded.

9:30 Tuck The Daughters back into bed then jam my toe on a doll bed in the hallway that was thrown out of Daughter 2's closet because the light in the hallway was out. Yeah, I don't understand that either.

9:45 Start an episode of Duck Dynasty and just when Si and Jace are about to confront Willie about an irksome issue with the reeds, come completely unglued when Daughter 1 pops into the living room and announces that she's finished the Percy Jackson book which she was able to read by turning on her closet light.

9:47 Have Brian to unscrew closet light.

9:55 Walk into the bathroom and scream because Daughter 1 is sitting on the toilet reading the next Percy Jackson book. Explain to Daughter 2 and Brian that I was just startled by Daughter 1 and that there are no other frogs in the house. Secretly hope that I'm right about the frogs; realistically know that I'm probably wrong! Probably? Hell. I know I'm wrong.

9:58 Announce that The Daughters are not allowed to get out of bed for the rest of the night.

9:58:32 Amend that they are not to get out of bed for the rest of the night unless the fire alarm goes off and then they can not only leave their beds, they can leave their rooms and scoot across the street to Mr. and Mrs. Bridges' house where they can, indeed play with their cat, Mouser, until the fire department shows up.

10:02 Tuck in the blankets for Daughter 1.

10:05 Tuck in the blankets for Daughter 2.

10:10 Turn on the CD player for Daughter 2.

10:12 Find the headphones for Daughter 1's MP3 player.

10:15 Change the CD for Daughter 2.

10:17 Check deadbolt on the doors and go to bed despite the continued giggling.

It never, ever, never changes.

Sign Of The Times

I have just returned from my fifteenth trip into Daughter 1's room this evening. We put her to bed about forty-five minutes ago. The first time she called me back to bring her a glass of water. She'd already had a large glass of water right before she went to bed. I know this for a fact because it was my large glass of water. I told her no. Goodnight. Sweet dreams. And as I walked out the door she called out her mantra, "You never let me have a drink of water!"

Over the course of this evening, I never let her pick out all of her outfits for the next two weeks. I never let her call her Nana just to tell her one little thing. I never let her rewash her hair and dry it with gel in it. I never let her bring the dog in to sleep on the foot of her bed. I never let her have a kitty. I never take her on an all-inclusive vacation in Puerto Vallarta. I never let her call her BFF to see if she'll bring her green bow tomorrow to school and the BFF will "bring her blue bow and they can do their hair together and be twins, but not really because one will be green and one will be blue."

I never let us paint our toenails the exact same color before bedtime. I never let her have a campout around the fire pit roasting marshmallows on a school night and singing "Camptown Races." Oh. And here's one for ya: I never taught her the words to "Camptown Races!" I never.

Never.

Never.

It wears me out.

I know, I know. I can hear all you good mommas saying, "Don't keep going in there. Say goodnight and ignore her." Oh. I forgot. It's just that easy.

I'll pause here to let you envision me rolling my eyes.

Honestly, when she was a baby and would fuss and cry out, it was much easier for me to ignore her. Basically because she was confined to her crib and had no way of marching herself into my office and scaring the bejeezes out of me while I was trying to write!

At any rate, now that she's older and has access to markers and papers and a street-facing window, I feel the need to check on her in case she really does need me. Or in case she's placed a "My mom never lets me out of my room" sign in her window. You know, again.

The policeman understood. He had an 8-year old daughter of his own. And he only lets her play with yellow markers anymore. Great suggestion, Officer McKelvey. Thank you very much, sir.

I'm sure that if I did ignore her, she'd learn to go to sleep that much faster, but it won't stop the constant use of the word "never."

Just last week I was listening to my Jillian Michaels CD while driving home from work. It was late, and I was tired, and I needed The Daughters to just be quiet so I could learn about balancing my time and prioritizing my health with Jillian. I drove us through McGaggles. I got The Daughters a healthy option: apple dippers—with caramel dipping sauce … geez! That audio book purchase was not wasted on this momma.

After we got our completely screwed up order and were on our way home, we drove past Burger Scream.

And Daughter 1, with her mouth full of McNuggets said, "Why don't you ever take us there?" I thought I had caught a break. At least she didn't say "never."

"I just got you a super-deluxe ecstatic meal, Girlie!" I reminded her, while still trying to listen to Jillian tell me how three hours of cardio would do wonders in clearing my mind. (Or was it three hours of waiting for hot fries would make me lose my mind?)

Then Daughter 1 dropped it: "Yeah, but you never take us there!" Oh. Sure. "Never."

I'm an educator. I have advanced degrees. I have studied child and adolescent development and learning styles and cognitive abilities and processes. I know brain-based research inside and out. However, I have yet to come across anyone who can fully explain this never complex that has invaded my child.

Wait. I said that wrong: I have "never" found anyone who can explain this to me!

I have paid very close attention to Daughter 1's "never" statements, and I'm the only one in the house who receives these sentiments. I mentioned to Brian that I found it not only odd but also frustrating that he never gets told that he never does whatever for Daughter 1.

And he, of course, had a ready explanation. His actions are always pleasing to Daughter 1 and my actions are always lacking. I reminded him of a few actions that would be lacking for him if he were never supportive of my cause again.

Finally, Daughter 1 is asleep. When I look at her sweet, peaceful face, I'm tempted to forget the "never" fight that we seem to be engaged in constantly. I wonder how I can ignore her constant requests, but I vow to myself that tomorrow is a new day. I will wake up and see to it that Daughter 1 has every single one of her needs met. And then some.

Then I grab a dark blue marker out of hiding and scribble this sign for her window: My mom Never does anything wrong.

It's a preemptive strike.

Actual Bedtime Prayer Of Daughter 2

Daughter 2: Dear God, Thank you for my health and my safety. Bless Momma and Daddy and our dumb dog, Bo and our poor dog, Daisy.

Me: What about your sister?

Daughter 2: Fine. And my poor, dumb sister.

Me: Daughter 2…

Daughter 2: Keep us all safe from harm and wake us in the morning early enough to get all the hot water before Sissy.

Me: Daughter 2…

Daughter 2: What? She makes me so sick! I just need a little bit of a time to shower and she takes up the whole time just standing there doing nothing and then when I get in it's cold and I don't get a shower. She bugs me! I just want hot water! Gah! Tomorrow morning if I beat her in the shower, I'm going to use all the shampoo and all the conditioner and all the hot water and then she'll learn that she needs to just be nice to me and leave me some hot water.

Me: Daughter 2 [I said as I fingered the little WWJD bracelet wrapped around her ankle] you're saying your bedtime prayers.

Daughter 2: Oh right. In Jesus' name, Amen.

The Holidays Are Always Around The Corner

I will be the first to admit that I kept a secret from Brian—back when we were first dating and he was just The Boyfriend. We began dating in June, and I was right smack dab in the middle of my secret.

I remember on our second date, before he came to pick me up, I scrambled to put the goodies I had just shopped for away in a closet so he wouldn't know. When he called me one morning, I just about broke my knee jumping over my bed to turn the stereo down. I knew that I'd be found out, and I knew that if I wanted this relationship to go places, I would have to be honest and let him know my secret eventually. I just wasn't sure the best way to tell him … or the best place … or the best time … so I kept my goodies hidden in the top of my closet and under my bed. My secret was safe.

Until that one fateful afternoon when he thought it would be romantic to just fling open my apartment door and surprise me. And he did. I was watching a movie—indulging myself in my own little secret world, and he burst right in. I remember he was carrying flowers—Ahhhh … back when I still got flowers. I guess this would be the time and place that I would be forced to share with him my secret.

He looked at the TV. Then he looked at me. He took a deep breath and he said, quietly and tentatively, "What … what is … what are you watching?"

I sighed and said, "*Christmas Vacation.*"

There. The truth was out.

I am a Christmas fanatic and I shop and celebrate year-round.

And it felt good to get it off my chest. I no longer needed to fear the shame of hiding this secret.

For years, I have celebrated Christmas from December 26 to December 25. I pick up wrapping paper for the next year at the after-Christmas sales and I start shopping for my list (checking it twice) in January. It's my goal, every year, to have my shopping completely completed before Thanksgiving.

To get in the mood, I listen to Christmas music in my minivan year-round. A tradition, I am proud to say, I'm passing onto my daughters. Don't call Human Services. They don't consider this abuse. And they told me during the last investigation that as long as I don't try to get them to harmonize with the Mormon Tabernacle Choir before The Daughters are in fifth grade, I am doing nothing wrong.

I hit the Black Friday sales to stock up on "incidental" presents. You know, when the neighbors bring over fudge on a crystal platter instead of chocolate chip cookies on a paper plate, then I'm prepared with those darling angel candlesticks (two for $5 before 4:00am at Hellmart) to gift right back at 'em. Then I spend the rest of the day decorating my house, snoozing on the couch, then yelling at the family for being too loud because they weren't up at three that morning buying fourteen turkey roasters ($8 each if you found them next to the blue light) to give out at Brian's office party.

I take my Christmas Card Picture (yes, that phrase does deserve to start with caps) right after Halloween and have the cards stamped and sealed and ready to put in the mailbox as we drive back north from Brian's folks home on Thanksgiving Day. Yes, I do wait until after Thanksgiving Day before I become outwardly manic about silver tinsel and snow-in-a-can. I do have some sense of normalcy.

Some.

I tell you all this so that you know I'm a fanatic. I am one hundred percent certifiable, loony over the Most Wonderful Time of the Year, which in my case, lasts all year long.

HOWEVER (yes, that word does deserve all caps) [Note from my Editor: Fine.], I am a little bit distraught that the day after Halloween, I turned on my favorite radio station (the one that plays Queen and Roberta Flack and Abba and KC and the Sunshine Band … all the good songs that I roller skated to … I mean, I would have roller skated to if I had been old enough. And despite what my friend Melinda says, I probably am not that old). I digress. So, I turn on my favorite radio station and my old buddy Bing is crooning about City Sidewalks and Snow Crunching, and I feel violated. That same day, I read the newspaper and see the Christmas ads are in full swing and I feel embarrassed. To think that Madison Avenue has invaded my private-year-round-red-sparkling-lights world and taken it before the public makes me feel exposed.

Please understand, I am not apologizing for my over-the-top fanaticism about all things reindeer and snowmen and fat-bearded men; I have nothing to apologize for. I do feel, though, that retailers and radio stations and marketing mongrels (yes, that's the word I intended to use) should apologize to all those people who screech into Hobby Lobby at 5:45 on December 24 looking for a few "last minute" things (which means they've got nuthin'). If I wish to watch *A Christmas Story* for twenty-four hours straight in the middle of August, that's my prerogative. And don't think I don't know where my less-than-supportive hubby hid that DVD after this year's run.

But, if there's just one person out there who wishes to not have twinkle-lighted garland tied around his or her neck as soon as the weather turns just the slightest bit not hot, then Madison Avenue should oblige. We all have our own time frames in our own minds: the smart ones (like me) will already have their shopping done by the time the two-for-the-price-of-one-plus-a-dollar ads run and won't be interested; and the daring ones (not like me) will be paying full-price for a bottle of Stetson for their great-grandpa on December 24 at 10:45pm at the mall.

It seems to me that their advertising buck would be better spent during the time it's intended and the savings could then be passed on to me (and you, too) whenever I choose to take it. Which would probably be January 15, the first payday after Christmas.

Really, do these ad execs have nothing better to think about than trees and red balls and German-chocolate calendars year-round? Because c'mon! Get a life.

Hey! That's what I do. Maybe I've missed my calling.

And I'll leave you with that because I just put my jack-o-lanterns away, and now I'm going to decorate my tree.

Actual Christmas Morning Convo

Daughter 1: [in an excited but hushed tone] Momma! Momma!

Me: [in a mumbled, half asleep grumbly, mumbly mumble] Wha-??

Daughter 1: Momma!

Me: Wha-? Who??!!?

Daughter 1: It's me, Momma! Daughter 1, Momma! Are you awake?

Me: O. M. G! [really, I said "O. M. G." I have not had much adult time recently]

Daughter 1: Mom! It's important. Please! Wake Up!

Me: OK! OK! What's the matter, Honey?

Daughter 1: I need to know what time it is. The clock in my room says 4:32. The clock on the microwave says 4:35 and your watch says 4:33. What time does your phone say?

Me: My phone? Ummm. [checking phone. Later, I'll be glad that she didn't ask me to lick the walls or do sit ups or something really weird because apparently, I'm pretty easily manipulated during the four o'clock hour]

Me: It's 4:38 on my phone, Honey.

Daughter 1: So, is it too early to get up?

Me: Get up?

Daughter 1: Get up out of bed. Well, I already am out of bed. Is it too early to get up and go see if Santa's been here?

Me: Who?

Daughter 1: Santa. Santa Claus. It's Christmas morning, Momma!

Me: Wha-?

Daughter 1: [slowly and deliberately as if speaking to a hard-of-hearting non-English speaker] Momma. Can. We. Please. Get. Up. And. Go. To. The. Living. Room. To. See. If. Santa's. Been. Here? [ends with a huge, big sigh]

Me: Wha-? No. It's too early.

Daughter 1: But, I cannot go back to sleep.

Me: Fine. Get in bed with us. And be quiet.

[another voice from the hallway] Momma?

[voice gets closer] Momma?

Daughter 2: Momma? Is it morning?

Me: Wha-?

Daughter 1: It's morning, but she won't let us get up yet.

Me: Who's talking here?

Daughter 2: But, Mooooommmmaaa!

Daughter 1: She won't. She's being stingy.

Me: Be quiet! It's too early to get up. Get back in bed.

Daughter 1: C'mon, Sister. Get in bed with us.

[Daughter 2 climbs in bed with us. Now there are a total of four people in our bed. Three of us are awake.]

Me: Girls, I'm pretty sure that Santa doesn't come to our house until 5:59, OK? So, be quiet and go back to sleep.

[silence for 4.3 seconds]

Daughter 1: What do you think we're gonna get?

Daughter 2: Maybe a pony! Or a four-wheeler! Or … I know! Moon Sand!

Daughter 1: Moon Sand… Yeah!

Me: Be quiet! If I hear your voices again, I will go start a fire in the fireplace and Santa won't be able to come down the chimney. So, just be quiet. Try to go back to sleep? Okay?

[silence for 57.4 seconds]

Brian: Babe?

Me: [ignoring him thinking that he'll be quiet and go back to sleep]

Brian: Babe?

Me: What?

Brian: What time is it?

Me: Wha-? Wha-? Why?

Brian: When did The Daughters get in bed with us?

Me: What?

Brian: Did you know The Daughters are in bed with us?

Me: Yes.

Brian: Why?

Me: [whimpering] Oh for the love. Why what?

Brian: Why are they in bed with us?

Me: They want to get up and see what Santa brought!

Brian: Oh. Well… Can we?

Me: Can we what?

Brian: Can we get up yet?

Give Me Thin Mints Or Give Me Death Or Give Me Death By Thin Mints

Every year when the little girls in brown, badge-laden sashes come knocking on my door, I always order four boxes of cookies: three boxes of peanut butter ones for Brian and The Daughters. And the fourth box? This box is for me. This box is full of heavenly goodness known as The Thin Mint. Up until this year, I could openly eat my box of Thin Mints whenever and wherever I wanted to. How'd I score such a privilege? Brian doesn't like Thin Mints. Doesn't like anything to do with mint. I married him anyway and—by the grace of God—we've not let this little oddity of his come between us. And up until this year, The Daughters have thought that they inherited their Daddy's disdain for all things minty.

This year, however, they were offered a Thin Mint cookie by a well-intentioned friend at basketball practice and discovered that they did not, in fact, gag as their Daddy had led them to believe would happen (and which I confirmed would likely be the case). This led The Daughters to come home and eat an entire box—my entire box—of Thin Mints. Well, they ate all but the ten that I devoured while driving home after getting the box of Thin Mints, of course. This, my friends was the first seasonal Girl Scout Cookie disaster.

Almost immediately, I raced to Hellmart, where I found an entire army of Girls Scouts ready to fill my order without hesitation or question. But, I am one smart momma. I bought three boxes. One for The Daughters to fight over, one for me to hide and eat on my own and one for me to put in the freezer and find as a wonderful surprise sometime in early summer when I would clean out the freezer looking for a place to stash the popcicles.

In no time at all, one box was completely gone. Then, The Daughters finished their box of Thin Mints. I resisted the urge to go get more of the minty goodness. I told myself that when summer rolled around and softball season was over and I actually cooked a meal instead of throwing together a sandwich or (when feeling especially Martha Stewart-y, grilled a quesadilla), I would be rewarded greatly for my efforts as a domestic engineer when I found the stashed box of frozen Thin Mints.

I was much impressed with my self-control after that. When I walked by the table of Girl Scout sugary-goodness as I entered my favorite grocery store, I politely declined their offers of more cookies. When the boxes were stacked at the register of one of our local grills, I informed the cashier that I had already purchased cookies and done my part. And judging by her sneer, she probably didn't care what I had previously purchased or whose part I had done as long as I left a decent tip! When I went to the mall to pick up the candles that were needed for the science project that was due by the end of the week, I thanked the Girl Scouts politely for asking me three times (twice not so politely—they were a persistent little troop!).

Driving in from the mall, as I opened the garage door, I was met with a scene that struck a most-sincere sadness in my mint-deprived soul: The Daughters were standing in front of the open freezer. I silently pleaded with the Girl Scout Cookie powers in the universe, "Please let them be looking for T-bones! Please let them be looking for T-bones!"

They were not looking for T-bones. They had found my own personal frozen stash. This, my friends, was the second Girl Scout Cookie Disaster of the season.

"Look, Momma! We found more Thin Mints! We're going to have a tea party and serve these Thin Mints!" They shrieked with giddiness at their discovery. I had to think fast if I wanted to save my Thin Mints from a certain un-appreciation at a childhood tea party.

"Ummm. Uhhh. If they're frozen, they don't taste good." I lied like Pinocchio.

"Nu-huh, Momma. We already tasted them. They tasted better than we remembered!"

"Oh! Um …" I stuttered, snatching the box from their grubby little hands, "These are expired! See? Says so right here."

"Momma, there's no date on the box. These things can last forever!"

Sigh. I couldn't outsmart the little cookie thieves. The best I could hope for was an invitation to the tea party. Or at least another reason to run back to Hellmart to grab a few more boxes to hide in the laundry room. If history and their piles of unfolded laundry are any indication, The Daughters will never go in there to look, right?

I Find No Happiness In My Closet

Recently, I read the bestselling book *The Happiness Project*. This book is the author's account of how she spent a year to boost her own happiness. With all due respect to the author, I'm not sure she has the correct definition of "happiness."

The book is broken down by months and she begins in January. First off, there's no starting anything happy in January. That's when everyone vows to lose weight, exercise more, eat healthy, wake up early—basically giving up the very things that make you happy. To paraphrase Tom Hanks in *A League of Their Own*, "There's no happiness in January."

I read on anyway, despite her oblivious attitude toward the dreary month.

Gretchen Rubin, the author, says that her own personal happiness project begins with cleaning out the closets. Blasphemy, I growled. I almost slammed the book shut and threw it into my closet. But, I had borrowed it from the library, and I knew that I'd never find it once it got lost in that black hole-ish pit that holds our clothes and shoes and everything else when company comes.

Then, I'd have to wait until January to clean out the closet and return the book. Can you imagine the fine the librarians would evoke? I'd have to clean out my closets and sell some clothes just to pay it off.

How in the world would cleaning out a closet make me happy? I mean, that's work. Work equals, um ... what's the word I'm looking for? Right, unhappy.

Gretchen's arguments for cleaning out the closet on the way to true happiness make sense, though. She is adamant that if one clears out the clothes that no longer fit, need repair or are damaged beyond salvaging, one is left with is, obviously, less clothes and fewer choices. Thus the morning routine of "What should I wear today?" is eliminated and one is happy because of this.

In my personal case, if I were to get rid of the clothes that no longer fit, need repair or are damaged beyond salvaging, I would be left with a pair of jeans (with a hole where the belt loops used to be attached. Holes are still fashionable, right?), a sweatshirt from Brian's college years (faded is in, right?) and a Christmas sweater that will never wear out since I only wear it once a year.

*Side note on the sweater—I have worn it to my family's Christmas get-together every year for the past nine years ... no one's ever said anything about it! But, when my Aunt Tattoo-Your-Lips wore her Christmas sweater (with a black dickey, none the less!) two years in a row, we've razzed her about it ever since. I love my family.

I did learn a little bit about how cleaning out a closet would make me happy. Gretchen—we're on a first name basis because I talked to her all while reading her book; well, talked to her book—Gretchen felt so great after cleaning out her closet that she then cleaned out her husband's closet as well. Now, we're onto something! As she cleaned out his closet, he sat on the bed, flippin' through *Real Simple*, sippin' sangria (I'm assuming).

Gretchen would hold up an article from his closet, he'd either give her a thumbs up or a thumbs down.

That, my friends, would make me happy. Finally, Gretchen was speaking to me.

No, no, no, no. I don't have any intention of cleaning out Brian's closet, but how happy would I be if Brian cleaned out my closet while I lounged and flipped and sipped?! I'd be as happy as a woman who had a husband who was cleaning out her closet for her—that's how happy I'd be.

Thank you, Gretchen. Great idea.

I approached Brian with my proposition because, after all, it would make me happy. He gave me a thumbs down.

To give Gretchen some credit, throughout the book, she reiterates time and again in her most verbose and redundant and bombastic and excessive and superfluous and copious way that we are not to copy her practices (no problem there, Gretch!). Instead, we should make our own happiness in whatever way works for us. And, 301 pages later, I would have to agree with you, Gretchen. We should make our own happiness.

My own happiness is going to start with staying up late, eating chocolate ice cream and watching The Twilight Saga—again! If vampires and werewolves don't make you happy, well, then, why don't you go clean out your closets?

Unsupervised Play dates Are The Only Way To Go

Recently, The Daughters have had several of their friends over quite a few times for "play dates." I love play dates. They give The Daughters a chance to play with their friends outside of school. They get to play games that require more than two players and none of the players have to be Brian or me. They get to make crafts and projects. They get to share jokes and books and riddles. They get to be creative and imaginative. They get to have all kinds of fun that they normally don't have when it's just their lousy family.

The biggest advantage to play dates, however, is that it gives me a chance to catch up on my DVR'd episodes of *Modern Family* and *Big Bang Theory*. Because of this little momma break, I thought play dates were a gift from heaven. Manna for the momma.

Then I got a magazine this week and one of the cover articles was "Games and Activities Everyone Will Love at Your Next Play Date!" I excitedly turned to this article thinking that if I had a really great activity, then not only could I get caught up on my shows, then maybe The Daughters and their friends would be so enthralled with their time together that I could sneak a Twinkie out of my secret stash and eat it without having to share

Then I read the article.

Apparently, the momma who wrote this article believes it's important to actually play with the kids during a play date.

To that, I say: WHA-?

I was appalled that this woman had totally missed the magic of a play date: Someone else to entertain your kids! Really. She should have asked me first; I'd have gladly turned her on as to how it was done here in the real world.

I giggle-snorted as I read the article. Brian paused the big televised game just long enough to ask me what I was giggling about. Actually he did not pause the game so much as he paused the commercial break during the game.

"This woman says that when her kids have play dates, she turns the TV off and plays with them!"

Then a little voice piped up and said, "CiCi's mom does that."

I jumped and just about peed my pants, "Wha-? Who said that?"

Daughter 2 said, "CiCi's mom always plays with us. Always. And there's a no-TV rule at their house when they have guests."

Under my breath, I murmured, "Does CiCi's mom also make you organic granola for a snack?"

And that sharp-eared little devil said, "She does! And I love it! It's my favorite healthy snack. Do you have the recipe?"

This was all news to me. My play-date world was crumbling down around my taco-flavored Doritos bag (hidden beside the recliner, so I wouldn't have to share).

That afternoon as FloJo, dropped her kids off to play with my kids, I asked her what she did when my girls came to her house. She quickly looked around and whispered, "Why? What'd they tell you?"

I related the highlights of the article to my friend and (thankfully) she was just as appalled as I was.

"But, when will I check Facebook if I'm playing Scrabble with them?" she cried.

"I know, right?" And I poured us both a glass of red wine (disguised in a coffee cup, so the kids wouldn't think they had to have a drink, too).

We agreed that it was a totally new concept to us and that probably our kids wouldn't really want us to play with them and their friends, right? Then she quickly excused herself because her crops are not going to plant themselves on Farmville, by golly.

I finished reading the article and then decided to give it a whirl. Really, how bad could it be to play with my own kids??

I should have known better than to drink and play. Really. I was about as out of touch as the momma who wrote the article was. Against, my better judgment, I engaged the kids anyway.

The first project I tackled was a bird feeder. Easy-peasy! I found Styrofoam cups, sunflower seeds, yarn and peanut butter. I gathered the items, and then quickly made myself a sunflower-seed-and-peanut-butter sandwich. I decided that maybe that wasn't the best project for us after all, especially since I had just used up all the peanut butter.

I think a game would fare better. I called the kids into the room and announced that we would play a game all together.

They announced that they were playing all together and started to leave the room.

"No! I mean with me!"

Daughter 2 said, “How about you call up CiCi’s mom and see if she’ll come play with us instead?” To which all the girls screamed, “Yeah!”

“Look,” I said, “I’m a good game player! What game do you want to play?”

Daughter 1 looked at the rest of the girls, they huddled then returned to me. Daughter 1 smiled slyly, and said, “We love hide and seek. I’ll be it!”

So, quickly, I secured my place in the corner of the linen closet. This was not an easy task because I had to wrestle with a king-size mattress cover. I was sure they would find me in no time because I had to move the suitcases into the hall in order to squeeze my dainty self into the hole. And then I held my breath and I waited.

You know what? It took very little time for me to realize this was kind of fun. I will admit that I giggled like a little girl on more than one occasion when time passed and I still hadn’t been found! I also giggled like a little boy when I passed gas and no one was around to scream, “Mooooooooooooommaaaaaaaaaa!”

And then my left foot went to sleep … and the sleepiness crept all the way up my leg and into my hip. I was able to grab my phone from my back pocket and check the time! I’d been in this closet for almost twenty minutes! I was totally winning. Unless …

Hey! I don’t think they’re playing right! I tried to stand up, but the whole left side of me was asleep. I tried to crawl out, but every time I did, I hit my head on the shelf so hard that I saw “Estrellas!” And then I heard Dora singing about “Estrellas.” And then I knew: The kids had duped me.

They had dumped me like a bad boyfriend.

They had left me stranded on the side of Play Date Road.

They were no more looking for me than I was able to stand up!

When Brian arrived at home, he knew something was up because they were singing Pink's "Rockstar" on the Wii Karaoke and eating my secret stash of M & M's. After what he considered to be his own personal game of Hide-And-Go-Seek with the wounded momma by hollering all around the closet without actually opening it, he removed the shelf from the closet and helped me get out.

"I was trying to be a good mom—like in the magazine!" I whimpered to him.

"You are a good mom," he assured me. "You just need to find a different magazine to take inspiration from." What a smart guy! And so sweet ... He immediately went out and got me a different magazine.

He brought home *Playboy*.

All Hail The Queen Of Hide And Seek

It wasn't long after that life-changing, leg-numbing experience that I did it. I won the world's best game of hide and seek and I didn't even try. Let's be clear about this: I didn't intend to play hide and seek with my family, as it's not one of my favorite games (anymore); but, to be clear, I did thoroughly enjoy the game, nonetheless.

It started off innocently enough, as these things do. I went back to my bedroom to read. I didn't announce it. I just got up, grabbed a magazine (not *Playboy* or any of those other obscene parenting magazines) and walked quietly and calmly to my bedroom and plopped down on our loveseat.

Really. The loveseat is a loveseat. That's not code for something you buy off Oxygen TV in the wee hours of the morning.

I had barely opened the front cover when I heard the first cry. It was Daughter 2.

"Momma! Momma! Come here, Momma!"

I had a very important lesson to teach: I could hop up and run to her assistance or I could sit here and let her hone in on her higher-order thinking skills by allowing her to come look for me instead of just hollering for me. Since I'm basically lazy, I chose option two.

I said nothing. Her voice didn't have an emergency-room tone to it, so I sat silently, slowly turning the pages. Besides that, Brian was in the living room watching

Baywatch reruns on Netflix. If it was really important, he could help them, right?

HAHAHAHAHAHAHAHAHA! I know! I sometimes crack myself up, too!

Daughter 2 continued her cries.

"Momma? Momma? Where'd you go? I said to come here! Where are you?" Then I heard her mumbling something to Brian. Good! He'd be able to help her and I could continue to read about how to de-clutter my house in five days or less. (Step 1: Get a match.)

Then she got dangerously close. She entered our bathroom and promptly hollered out, "She's not in here, Dad! Where else do you think she is?"

At this point, Daughter 1 got involved swearing she could find me easy-breezy because she knows everywhere I would be because she's smarter than Daughter 2. And smarter than Brian as far as that goes. So there. And on some days, she's pretty much smarter than I am as well. No brag, just facts.

I had a few more minutes of time by myself as The Daughters fought over who was smarter. Finally Brian stepped in and said he was smarter. And he was trying to watch this one part where the lifeguards run down the beach to save someone, so would they kindly hold the yelling down to a dull roar.

Together, Daughter 1 and Daughter 2 went room to room calling out my name. Still, I sat silently on the loveseat; I even pulled my feet up off the floor. I'm not sure why; I just did. I felt as if I were in a bathroom stall skipping class. Not that I have ever skipped class, of course.

The Daughters came as far as the edge of the loveseat, but didn't walk into the alcove where I was. I held my breath and they walked on, calling my name. I heard them check every closet in our hallway and even in their bedrooms. I heard Daughter 1 command Daughter 2 to go check to see if the minivan were still in the driveway. As if I could get away with actually leaving the premises without a major uprising … or could I? An important point for this momma to ponder.

The Daughters returned to our bedroom and I heard them throw back our shower curtain and scream, "A-ha!" to … an empty shampoo bottle and two damp washrags. Then Daughter 2 checked the cabinet under the sink and above the toilet. I love that girl for thinking that I was small enough and light enough to fit into either one of those spaces.

Still, through my tears of joy over Daughter 2's vision of a dainty and petite momma, I remained silent.

By this time, The Daughters were beginning to get seriously worried and pester Brian to the point that he had to flip down the screen on Pamela Lee Anderson and Yasmine Bleeth and look for his reality: me. Besides that, it was almost time for dinner and he wasn't entirely sure what temperature the oven should be set on for our gourmet frozen pizza. Nothing but the best for my family.

"Honey! Where are you?" He hollered; I said nothing and listened as he told The Daughters, "Don't sweat it — she's here somewhere. Where's she going to go anyway?"

Say Wha-? I could go anywhere I wanted! I'm an independent woman. I make my own choices! And today, I choose to stay home and mess with my family, thank you very much.

The trio made their way back to our bedroom, and I held my breath. Brian scanned the room, looking right over the loveseat, and then they exited, thinking I must have gone outside. As I watched them race into the backyard from the bedroom patio doors, I raced into the living room and lounged on the couch, thumbing through my magazine.

Within five minutes the three blind mice were traipsing back into the house where they discovered me flipping the pages of *Woman's Weekly*, having the time of my life.

Daughter 1 was mad, demanding, "Where have you been?"

Daughter 2 was near tears, "Don't ever leave me again, Momma!"

Innocently, I explained to them that I'd been right on that spot all along! I had no idea what they were talking about. "I heard you calling!" I explained, which was the truth, I just didn't answer.

Brian was delusional; "Pamela would never play this kind of joke on our family!"

I laughed right out loud, "That's because Pamela isn't smart enough, my dear."

The Best Dad Quotes

"You're such a cheap and easy date. I mean that in a good way."

"Do you wanna marry me? For real?"

"I'll clean up after dinner if you do the dishes."

[as he sits in our truck cradling his golf clubs and smoke pours out of our house] "Run back in and get our pictures!"

"I didn't hear the baby cry last night."

"Let me rewind this so you can watch this guy's poker hand."

"I wasn't like that as a kid. That I remember anyway."

"Did you follow my mom's recipe for this? Because I think you did something wrong."

"Am I accidently wearing your shorts?"

[while watching A League of Their Own] "I am not crying."

Sloppy Joes Spawn Creativity

Brian and The Daughters' incessant need to be fed on a daily basis is a whole 'nother source of summer stress for me. Almost every single day as I haul my tired self out of bed in the ~~morning,~~ ~~late morning~~ sometime before noon, they'll begin the whining for food. They're as needy as stray dogs. Now that I think about it, that may be why I'm reluctant to actually feed them.

Oh, please. Y'all know that I do, indeed, feed my family but so far, after seven weeks of summer, I have yet to feed them anything they actually like. Just last week, I made Sloppy Joes. Daughter 2 is normally a big fan of Sloppy Joes. She'll even eat leftover Sloppy Joes. Have you ever heard of such a thing as a child who eats leftovers? I decided to be a playful momma and as I picked up Daughter 2 from her softball sliding camp, I told her that for dinner that evening, we were going to have Sloppy Daughter 2's. Get it? I swapped out the name "Joe" for "Daughter 2." Clever, right?

It was clever only to me. During the fifteen-minute drive home, after I announced the serving of Sloppy Daughter 2s, I heard no less than 7,328 cries of "It's not fair!" Apparently, Daughter 2 doesn't like Sloppy Daughter 2s. She only likes Sloppy Joes. As I pulled into the driveway, I turned in my seat to face Daughter 2.

"Look," I said, "I was being funny. I made Sloppy Joes and just changed the name to make a joke." I spoke calmly and coolly and refrained from ripping my immediately greying hair right off my head.

"It doesn't matter. I don't like Sloppy Joes anymore," Daughter 2 confessed.

I snarled my lip and questioned the little traitor, "Since when?"

"Since you changed the name." I sighed and then explained in no uncertain terms that she could eat it or not.

She chose the "not" option.

The next morning as I overslept and almost didn't get her to bike-riding-cheerleader camp in time, I yelled at her as I brushed my teeth that she needed to make sure she had on underwear (yes, in our house, it needs to be said) and to grab something for breakfast.

We breathlessly pulled out of the driveway and I turned to ask Daughter 2 if she had grabbed breakfast.

"Yes, momma," she said sweetly and innocently, "I ate leftover Sloppy Joes."

"What?" I said not even trying to hide the utter confusion in my voice.

"I found Sloppy Joes in the fridge and I had one for breakfast."

Consciously not gritting my teeth, I explained to her that the leftover Sloppy Joes were from last night, when she refused to eat them because I had called them Sloppy Daughter 2s.

"Really?" she asked. I nodded my head as I sped toward whatever bike-riding-cheerleader camp.

"Huh!" Daughter 2 exclaimed, "I guess I do like them no matter what you call them."

"I told you that," I sighed.

She pondered my profound words as she stared out the window. “Did you also tell me to put on my underwear?” I nodded in exasperation.

“Well, Momma,” she said, “We may have to run home real quick.”

Binders, Erasers and Rulers; Oh, My!

The Daughters and I went shopping for school supplies. It's always a bittersweet time for me: Sweet because it means that The Daughters have to go back to school and their teachers get to share the zaniness that I have been living for the past twelve weeks. Bitter because it means that I have to go back to school and share the zaniness that every other parent has been living for the past twelve weeks. How many days until Fall Break?

Daughter 1 has long been a reader and has always taken her own list of supplies and I just turn her loose and swipe my card when she's done. This year was no different.

Daughter 2, however, she's my baby! I have always treated her as such. When we go get school supplies, her baby-ness is especially evident as we pick just the right color of folders and the exact type of scissors … together.

This year, my friends, the tide has turned. [sniff, sniff] Daughter 2 has had an amazing start to her education; she's had an awesome pair of preschool and kindergarten teachers. (Thank you, Mrs. Flick and Mrs. Schaper!) And? And? When we went to Hellmart this past week, Daughter 2 said she wanted to get her own school supplies. [sniff, sniff] She didn't need me to read her the list.

She read it herself. [sniff, sniff, BAWL! BAWL!]

Again, [insert sarcasm] thank you Mrs. Flick and Mrs. Schaper.

Oh for heaven's sake—she's just growing up too fast. With this growing up comes many, many changes. Ultimately this means, I'm going to have to find a different way to write "Rum" on my shopping list.

As The Daughters wandered through the school supply aisles, I stood at the glue stick display and monitored. That's what I'd been reduced to-a monitor.

Truthfully, I had no problem with anything Daughter 1 put into the cart. She's a rule follower. If her list said she needed twelve glue sticks that were only manufactured in Spokane, WA, she'd be online finding the nearest dealer because that's what the list said to get.

Daughter 2? Not so much. Daughter 2 is a heart-follower. Basically, that's an endearing way of saying she does whatever she wants. Case in point: Her first grade list clearly states "classic markers." Daughter 2 brings me the pack of markers that has pink and turquoise in it.

"No, honey. These are not classic markers," I say, pointing to the word on her list.

"What does classic mean?"

"It means basic or original."

"Pink is a basic color, Momma."

"Well, kinda," I say hesitantly … but it's too late, she's already heard the weakness in my voice and dumps the markers in the cart and heads back out.

Next, she brings in the three-subject spiral, even though she clearly needs the one-subject spiral. She tells me that she is probably going to do a lot of writing in first grade and will need more pages. Plus, it's in plaid and she can't find a single-subject notebook in plaid. Now I ask you: How can you argue with such logic?

Through the course of our back-to-school shopping, she gets three boxes of tissues instead of two because she knows a lot of kids with allergies. She gets 64 crayons instead of 48 because she's "a big colorer." We end up purchasing a glue gel instead of glue sticks because gel won't dry out like the sticks will. And even though the list didn't specially ask for a compass and protractor kit, she's pretty sure it was an oversight and she needed it. And really? What first grader doesn't need a compass and protractor kit? I'm a professional educator and truthfully? I'm not even sure how to use these items.

Finally, to top it all off, we needed a backpack. But as Daughter 2 says, "Everyone has a regular ol' backpack." So, we ended up with a sparkly, silvery-sequined shoulder bag.

There. We're ready to go back to school.

Yeah, yeah, yeah. I hear all of you fellow teachers mumbling that the list was created with specific items in mind. I get that. And, while Daughter 2 was admiring The Jonas Brothers on a three-ring cover, I was quickly swapping out her choices for the correct choices. Why? Because I, like Daughter 1, am a rule-follower. And Daughter 2—though a free thinker—is a bit scatter brained and completely forgot what she did or did not pick out by the time we got home with our back-to-school loot.

Rest assured, though all you hippie-dippie sympathizers out there, we did keep the sparkly, silvery-sequined shoulder bag.

I'll Give You Something To Do...

All summer long, I heard the horrible kid's cuss words: "I'm bored." I hear all the mommas out there groan in agreement. I battle The Daughters each summer to get them to stop saying "I'm bored" despite the fact that we have an in-ground pool, two dogs, a swing set, a game system, a laptop and a desktop, two bikes, two scooters, four pair of skates, a piano, two easels, approximately $23,402 worth of toys, and 423 books. On or about the second day of summer, they start in with their "I'm bored" battle cry and they stop approximately two hours before school starts back.

All I have to do is recognize the preceding sigh and my eye starts twitching and I start rattling off dozens of things they could do. Then I cover my ears and sing, "Lalalalalalalalalalala!" so as to not actually hear them say the dreaded words because I am certain—beyond the shadow of any doubt—that if I have to hear those words uttered just one more time, I'll begin each morning by pouring tequila on my Special K. What? That's not right. I'll probably start skipping my Special K and just shooting the tequila. Feel free to join me. As I like to say, "It's better to shoot tequila than to shoot people."

Good news, my friends: I secured 264 dozen things to keep The Daughters not only busy but also exhausted throughout their summer days. In fact, it kept them so tired and so occupied, that they couldn't even utter the word "bored." Sigh; I have seen the Promised Land.

But it was not an extended stay in Utopia. Alas, with children, it never is.

Children? Did I say children?

Let's go back to this afternoon when the almost-comatose Daughters were grateful for the down time to relax. They were sprawled across the couch, their little tongues hanging from their mouths, their little eyes glazed over. Journey was softly singing through the stereo speakers, and the house was almost heavenly.

Almost.

For, this afternoon, as the rain poured from the heavens onto our 136 degree grounds, and our air conditioner shut off for the first time in about forty days and nights (the thermostat is set at 83), Brian sat in his recliner and sighed.

"What's up, Buttercup?" I lovingly asked Brian with a smile on my face and a twinkle in my eye (or something like that).

And then ... my serene nirvana crashed. Brian, sighing again, said, "I'm bored."

The Daughters, even though they were barely alert, they were aware enough of this dastardly utterance by the man they were afraid would become a distant and fond memory at the hands of their Momma and they, pressing their backs against the wall, scooted to their rooms to huddle and pray on their beds. No, not really. They hid in their closets. They know the wrath that uttering "that phrase" can bring down upon the sayer, thus sayeth Momma.

With my brow furrowed and my voice about three octaves below normal, I whispered to my blissfully ignorant and not-so-blissfully bored husband, "Wha-???"

With yet another sigh, Brian spoke the second most popular kid's cuss word, "I have nothing to do."

Now, I'm pretty sure he'll not utter those words again after he figures out how to get the dismantled recliner off of his body, but in case he does, here's a small list of "things to do in case you are bored." (Feel free to steal the list and post it on your fridge in case you have a bored Dad-like character living in your home.)

1. Momma will never turn down a pedicure-complete with foot rub. Never. Ever never. This can be given by you or by the nice little Asian woman down at Elite Toes and Aquarium Supplies. Doesn't matter: Just produce the pedicure. Even if this doesn't cure your boredom, it will relax the Momma in your life so that she won't want to go postal on your bored ass.

2. Even though the bathrooms are cleaned with some regularity (at least once a month for his poker games.), as soon as just one person uses the facilities again, the bathrooms are dirty again. Clean them. The cleaning supplies are located under the dirty sink. Where they've always been. They're not hiding. It is okay for you to snoop around and find these easy to use supplies—just find them. Then use them.

3. I really didn't place a special "coating" on the tabletops and other flat surfaces of our home just so The Daughters could practice their penmanship or art skills. They're dusty. Dust them off. Again, the cleaning supplies have not moved since I used them last. Under the sink, dude. Find them. Use them.

4. I will always sit and watch the following s with you: *Mamma Mia, Grease, Moulin Rouge* and the *PBS John Denver Special.* Bonus points if you stay awake.

Extra bonus points if you stay awake and don't snort while watching them.

5. And, if you sing along with the previously mentioned DVDs when appropriate, you'll most likely not be bored when we go to bed tonight. [wink, wink, nudge, nudge] Don't know the words? Don't worry; I'll put the sing-along-words on the screen. You're welcome.

6. Despite the abundance of frozen dinner packages you'll find in the trash during certain times of the year, dinner doesn't cook itself. But you certainly can cook dinner—any time. Hey! I'll even be thrilled if you just microwave dinner. Or pick up pizza. Either way, you're not bored, and momma is happy.

7. Even though I've read *Eat, Pray and Love*, I didn't quite get into it as much as everyone else did. Maybe if someone would read it to me, I'd totally get what the fuss is all about. Maybe. At the very least, it'd be a good time to doze. Besides, I love the sound of your voice. That is unless your voice is complaining of your bored state of mind.

8. That weird looking thing in the closet on which we drape our jackets really doesn't exist to keep our hoodies conveniently located toward the front of the closet. It actually was created to vacuum our carpets. Unfortunately it needs a person to operate it in order for it to fulfill its mission in our home. And despite your objections that you don't know how to use it, it's on-the-job training. So, get busy, Bucko.

9. We have an iron. We have an ironing board. They are dusty and appear to be just for show, but they are still in working order. I have been telling myself that the wrinkled look is in. It's not. You could iron our clothes.

Bonus: You'd become my mom's favorite son-in-law with this little act alone. And,

10. Did I mention that I love foot rubs? I did? Good. Don't forget this option.

The DIY Dad Or How I Fixed A Toilet With A Hammer

When we bought our current house about three years ago, there were quite a few cosmetic things that we wanted to do: Paint walls, put in new floors, attach mirrors to the ceiling. I jest, of course. The mirrors were already up there. It's what sold us.

The kind, elderly gentleman from whom we bought the house was a handyman himself and had added several things, like bookshelves and homemade towel racks. Two days before closing, when the front toilet more or less exploded, flooding the entire house, we learned that he was not so much a handyman as he was a tinkerer.

So, off and on, throughout our three years here, Brian and I laugh about the tinkerer. And by laugh, I mean cuss like sailors as we're cleaning up the mess that has been created by his well intentioned but not-securely executed home "improvements."

About six weeks ago, the master toilet encountered its share of troubles. Did I say six weeks ago? I meant six months ago. The problem was very simple and wouldn't flood our home. The pusher needed to be replaced and the chain on the flapper-dealie was shot. Basically, the toilet wouldn't flush without someone reaching in the back box-place and pulling the flapper by hand. Simply put, we needed to replace the pusher and chain dealie.

Go ahead and be utterly impressed with my use of such technical terms. It was an easy fix.

We didn't need no stinkin' professional to do this job. I asked Brian if he would kindly fix the toilet. He said he would and promptly removed the top from the back box so it would be easier for me to pull the flapper. He's a funny man. He's a funny man who often sleeps in his recliner.

Now, Brian takes issue when I ask him to do something and then I end up doing it myself. He says I don't give him enough time to actually do whatever it is that I need him to do. Basically, he says that if I ask him to do something, I should let him do it.

Very well then. On this particular instance of toilet flapper-chain issues, I would respect his wishes. Blah, blah, blah.

But, remember when our toilet first broke? That's right, six months ago.

Good. We're all on the same page.

Every once in a while, I'd ask Brian to fix the toilet and I'd get a myriad of responses:

"I'll go get the parts next week."

"I don't have the time right now."

"The World Series of Poker is on."

"We have two other toilets."

"What's wrong with reaching into the back box?"

"Are you enamored with plumbing and why aren't you wearing that little red, lacy thing?"

I could fix it. I knew exactly what I needed to get at the home improvement wonderland just down the road. I knew exactly how to change out the pusher and the flapper chain. But, it was a matter of principle. Brian said I needed to give him time; therefore, I was giving him time. Too much time. While I wanted the toilet fixed, I really wanted the power of holding it over his head more. I really, really wanted that power—bad!

Last week, however, my hand was beyond chapped. I went to the wonderland and had a very nice salesperson (Larry) who knew exactly what I was talking about when I said I needed to purchase a pusher and a flap chain. My pal Larry hooked me up and I was on my way home.

I honestly attempted to change out the parts. I even knew how to turn off the water. That's about as far as my wimpy muscles would allow me to go. The tinkerer, who lived here before us, had not only tightened the pusher when he replaced it, but he tightened it while it was not straight. Then, he applied some sort of adhesive to ensure it would stay crookedly in place. Therefore, it was "pert-near" (a Larry term) impossible to get off.

Damn it! No. Damn it all! Wait. Damn it all straight to hell!! My home-improvement independence would be short-lived! I was going to have to ask Brian for his help. My ego needed an out. I didn't want to ASK. I had basically been begging for six months. So, I paraded myself right between Brian and the All-Poker-All-The-Time channel and headed to the garage. I grabbed the biggest hammer we had and paraded myself right back again.

"Hey! What are you doing?" He questioned pausing the TV just after it was revealed that Smoothy Joe had a pair of fours in the pocket up his river. Or whatever.

"Me?" I queried in my best, innocent voice. OK, fine, it's my only innocent voice. "I'm fixing the toilet."

Before I could say "flapper chain," Brian was up racing to the bathroom where after twenty minutes of grunting and five minutes of cussing the tinkerer, I had a real-live flushing toilet again. I cried. I cried because as I sat down to use my fully-functioning toilet, I discovered the toilet paper roll was empty. Damn it all to hell—again and again!

The Tooth Fairy Drops $20s

FloJo, and I both have two daughters who are the same ages. As with any little girls of any age, they like to have sleepovers. Usually, because FloJo is just so nice, she'll suggest that one of us take Daughters 1 and the other takes Daughters 2.

Occasionally when we're feeling especially generous or tipsy or forgetful, or a combination thereof, we'll take all four girls for a sleepover and give the other momma a night to herself. We sometimes even let our husbands stay when that happens. Usually we'll go out and have a glass of White Zin and eat fancy specials at fancy diners and not have to cut up anyone's food or sop up anyone's spilled strawberry soda. And then we'll text the one with The Daughters a simple: Thx! And the one with The Daughters will text back: Bring me sangria in a go-cup!

Our preference, however, is that we'll divide and pretend to conquer. Both of our first borns have been dubbed "High Maintenance." Their initials really do spell out H.M. and they really are high maintenance. They are both smarter than I am and are constantly thinking and doing and needing things like self-rising yeast or chlorine tablets or fifteen dog leashes because they always have "a really great idea." And when we don't have an ounce of melted 10K gold at our fingertips, we are treated to eye rolling times two and sighing in stereo.

The Daughters 2 have been dubbed "The Crazies" because, well, they just are. They're much easier to keep because they usually want to play by themselves, and they want the mommas to stay the heck away from them. No witnesses. This, my friends, is an easy night. Let The Crazies lock themselves in the bathroom with a tub full of bubbles and Barbies and call it a night.

This past weekend, I drew the long stick and I kept The Crazies. High Maintenance went with FloJo, where they made perfume and carried luggage up and down the stairs. See? High Maintenance.

The Crazies, on the other hand, played vampire and rich girl … taking turns being the vampire to be fair. (Maybe I'm a bit into *Twilight* too much.) And while playing vampire, they discovered that they may or may not have loose teeth. First, I checked my crazy's tooth. It was not loose in the least. Next, I checked FloJo's crazy's tooth … just a smidgen bit of looseness.

Then The Crazies were off again! They ran to the bathroom and shut the door. I—like any good momma—settled in to watch Literal Music Videos on YouTube. [Note from my editor: I love "Mullet With A Headlight!"] [Note from me: You and me both. Where have you been all my life?]

An hour later, I'm only slightly embarrassed to admit, The Crazies emerged. My Crazy said, "Momma, I think I can get her tooth yanked out if I use a pair of scissors." I chased them down (after finishing watching a literal video of "Total Eclipse of the Heart") and put a stop to that nonsense. For that exact moment only.

The evening progressed, and The Crazies got into pink underwear to sleep in (just pink underwear) and I turned off the lights. At 11:15, The Crazies came bursting into our bedroom—where, thankfully, Brian and I were still decent … no, presentable … no, covered (that'll work!). And FloJo's Crazy held out her little hand, which contained a little tooth. The Crazies had done it. They had extracted a not-yet-ready to be pulled tooth without tools (that I know of) or anesthesia (to my knowledge).

Then, they promptly lost the tooth. It landed somewhere on my carpet, which was last vacuumed when it was installed about three years ago.

After we called FloJo and told her of this milestone, I asked her if she wanted the Tooth Fairy to visit at our house or would she make an appearance the next night at FloJo's house. We decided that if Brian and I could remember (we have a track record for forgetting—just ask my half of "High Maintenance") then the Tooth Fairy would fly in that night.

And she did. She left $20. I told FloJo's Crazy that the Tooth Fairy always left a $20 … sometimes even a $50.

I think I may have just pushed her into the High Maintenance group. Later the next day, FloJo called and said she had gotten the story of exactly how the tooth had been removed from the mouth.

It seems that FloJo's kid placed the bed sheet in her mouth and tucked the rest of the sheet under the mattress. Daughter 2, climbed on top of her desk, which is adjacent to her bed. When FloJo's kid had her teeth firmly clamped down on the sheet, Daughter 2 jumped from her desk to the bed, which jerked the sheet-and the tooth-from FloJo's kid's mouth.

"Holy Cow, FloJo!" I said, "I'm so sorry! Are you ever going to let her come over again?"

"OH, hellz yeah, baby," FloJo practically screamed in my ear, "This momma's gotta get a break from Crazy every once in a while."

Truer words have never been spoken.

The Baby Maker Goes Public

I got myself a brand new IUD put in and I'm not taking this sucker out until the gyno announces my ovaries are shrunken up and useless.

Wait. Why did I say "brand new?" Like, can you even buy used IUDs? Would you pick one up on Craigslist or something? Are they on the Free list? If they were, would I even consider getting a "gently used" IUD? And if I did consider it, how much money would I save? Just how cheap am I when it comes to my IUDs?

What?

Let me start again:

I got myself an IUD put in and I'm not taking this sucker out until the gyno announces my ovaries are shrunken up and useless.

But …

Every once in a while, I like to yank Brian's chain and ask him if we should have more babies. This usually gives me the opportunity to see how red his ears turn in relationship to his blood pressure and pulse. Eventually, I may have The Daughters use this for a science fair project. But, the baby subject does come up quite often at our house.

We have several babies in our lives right now: Baby Kathryn from church, whom we love to entertain during "silent" prayer; Baby Bree, our cousin who can—no lie—recite the offensive line of the Dallas Cowboys; and Baby Whitley, our cousin who has the crazy knack for finding water and falling into it. Then there's Baby CC, who can cry at the mere sight of Brian.

In addition to all these babies, we have lots of pregnant women in our lives as well right now. We are waiting the arrival of Baby Maggie any day now; Baby Bode will make his debut in November; and Baby Naomi will be coming in December. With all these babies in our lives, two things were bound to happen.

1. The Daughters would start asking questions; and
2. The Momma (that's me) would get baby fever.

Let me just reiterate yet again (but, I'm sure, not for the last time): We are having no more babies. NO MORE BABIES COMIN OUTTA MY WOOWOO!

Prior to becoming Daddy and Momma, Brian and I had worked out a little plan. If our babies turned out to be girls, I would answer all their questions about "girly" stuff. If our babies turned out to be boys, Brian would fill them in on all things manly. So, when these babies all started popping into our life, questions started popping into our conversations. And The Daughters are girls, so I got to field the questions. Immediately I knew that plan was a crock.

Daughter 1 informed me one day in the van as I was driving across a bridge—I thought we'd meet the maker that very instant—that she knew how the babies got out of the momma's tummies. And, anatomically, she was correct. So, I confirmed that yes, indeed, that's how they got out. Then she threw me for a doozy. "But, Momma," she asked thoughtfully, "How do they get in there?"

Hmmm. She was only 7. To what extent do I share details with her? And with her 5-year-old sister sitting next to her? I know. I'll just turn up the radio. I cranked up the oldies station and let Madonna belt out, "Like a Virgin"-that should sufficiently distract them, right?

As I reached for the radio knob, Daughter 2 swooped in to my rescue: "Duh!" she exclaimed in her best Hannah Montana voice, "Babies get in their momma's tummies because of God." And to that I said, "Amen." You can't argue with an answer like that, so I didn't … and that concluded my "talk."

End scene.

I knew I had been successful because The Daughters were quietly contemplating my words of wisdom in the back seat. I was content to just let them share their musings with each other and just listen in. Then Daughter 1 called me back into the conversation and she drew her big guns: "I know you and Daddy have sex."

Whoa. Did she …? Well, yes she …! Ummm ... Excuse me while I drive the van over this bridge.

When did she discover this? How did she know for sure? Did she inherit the voyeur tendencies of Brian, who likes to watch Oxygen late at night when he can't sleep? And why didn't she say something when she discovered us "wrestling?" Also, why don't we have a lock on the door?

These questions all went unanswered as I wept and Daughter 1 kept right on talking.

"And I have sex," Daughter 1 continued. Oh. My. Gracious, I thought, this is what a stroke feels like. She kept on, "And so does Sissy. That makes three girls sexes in our family and one boy sex."

Whew. An early grave had been averted for Momma.

Still, being around babies and seeing The Daughters get so worked up with all the babies (and pregnant bellies) in our lives right now does give me a touch—just a touch—of baby fever. Luckily, just when I think I can feel my ovaries jumping clear up to my almost-lactating chest, the nearest baby will have something ooze out of her diaper or will shove a cheese ball in his ear or puke on a new leather sofa or throw a fit when I won't buy M & M's (wait … that was Brian). And that baby fever goes right out of my sagging and flabby body.

Just to clear this up once again: Brian and I are NOT having any more babies. There are two very good reasons for this: 1. If we had another child, we'd have to break away from our man-on-man defense and run a zone defense. This, my friends, would be the end of the game, as we know it. And, as we know it, we're probably not going to end up winning anyway. And 2. The Daughters are professional children. Brian and I are amateur parents (at best).

But, I still like to yank his chain when I get a chance to—keeps his ticker in shape.

The Time-Traveling Conundrum

This weekend, we loaded up the minivan and headed south to Brian's childhood home to visit with his folks. If you MapQuest this trip, you'll discover that it takes approximately three hours and thirty-three minutes. Twelve years ago, Brian and I took this same trip and could make it in just under three hours. We were young and fast and nothing could stop us.

Then we had kids.

I remember the first time we traveled with Daughter 1 on this journey. She was six weeks old and the trip took us about four and a half hours. I was nursing, so we'd have to stop and nurse. Then stop and let me eat. Then stop and let me go to the bathroom. Then stop and change a diaper. We couldn't wait until I was no longer nursing. (Back off, nursing moms of America! I did it; I enjoyed it; I hated doing it while traveling.)

Then along comes Daughter 2. The trip now takes about five hours because we now have to stop and nurse. Then stop and eat. Then stop and let Daughter 1 try to go potty all by herself on the stinky, messy potty at the Choctaw gas station. And we couldn't wait until we were no longer nursing and / or potty training.

The Daughters are now both in school; nursing and potty training are now things of the past. You would think that our trip could now take the three hours and thirty-three minutes that MapQuest offers. To that, I would like to say, "Bull shit, MapQuest! I cry Bull shit!"

I would also suggest that MapQuest hire some mommas for their consultation team so we could get realistic times.

Let me break this trip down for ya.

We load the minivan and pull out of the neighborhood. We just get onto the highway when Daughter 1 discovers that she's left her glasses at home. We turn around and are a block away from the house when she discovers that she didn't leave them at home after all. They were in her drink holder. But now, Daughter 2 has to go to the bathroom, so we head home and use the bathroom and start our trip again.

We just get out of town when Daughter 1 thinks she might have to go to the bathroom as well. We tell her that she'll just have to wait because there's not a bathroom around. Daughter 1 believes that whining the phrase "Now! I have really gotta go now," repeatedly will make a bathroom magically appear in the middle of pastureland. So, we detour at the next available exit and find a bathroom. Where we also get drinks … because these twenty miles we've traveled from home have sure made us thirsty. And because Brian doesn't think it's "right" to use a bathroom at a convenience store without making a purchase of some sort. But, he does think it's perfectly fine to fart in a car with the windows sealed shut and the outside temperature is twenty-eight degrees. He thinks it's even more acceptable if he can do it silently.

Where was I? Oh yeah … twenty miles from home.

We get back onto the highway and land in the big city right at rush hour in the middle of construction season behind a church bus driving seniors to the pumpkin patch. And now I have got to go to the bathroom. So does Brian, but he'd never admit that's why he's shaking his knees and drumming the steering wheel. We pull into the next visible gas station because we are "close to empty" (as much as half a tank is close to empty) and fill 'er up and drain 'er out … get it? That's a good one, huh?

We get back on the highway and The Daughters begin to feel a bit hungry. Then a lot hungry. Then they begin the moaning and whining. Never fear! I packed our dinner. This will save us about forty-five minutes eating in the car. Brian pulls over and I climb to the back of the van only to discover that our "car picnic" is still on the counter at home. We pull into the next clown-endorsed eatery and order the fattiest and friediest things on the menu. We use the restroom, refill our drinks and head on down the highway.

By this time, it's starting to get dark. This means The Daughters want to color, of course. So they begin fighting over crayons and coloring books and who has more light on their side of the van. Then—BAM! No. Not a blowout. A blowout would have been welcome. My friends, it's a full-blown, knock down, drag-out crayon war. There's screeching and pulling and throwing. Finally, I take the crayons and the coloring books into the front with me and Brian gives the girls a "tongue" time-out: For the next five miles, no one is allowed to talk. I started to congratulate him on a genius parenting idea, and he shushed me.

Since The Daughters will obviously implode if they have no release, they begin kicking the seat. This is where Brian channels all Dads who have gone before him and threatens to … say it with me now … "Turn this car around!" Which causes the girls to laugh, because, really? We're never going to turn this or any other car around. If we turned the car around, we'd have to relive the whole ordeal only in reverse! The laughing from the hyenas in the middle seats then causes the girls to have to go to the bathroom. So, we stop. Again. We're now three hours into the journey and not even half way there.

Right after leaving that particular gas station, we discover that we've left our turnpike pass in the other vehicle. Our next mission? We have to find an ATM to get cash. Then, we have to wait in line with all the other losers, I mean, out-of-state travelers, who must also pay cash.

We fight over the CD selection approximately 9,000 times before we settle on Christmas music, which causes Brian to plug in his own MP3 and tune us out. I like when he does this though, because I think it's hysterical to record him singing along to Hannah Montana.

We stop to go to the bathroom again. Then return to the bathroom because someone (I won't tell you that it was the male in this family) left his phone in the bathroom, which is really weird considering he didn't even have to go potty when we pulled in. It's also weird because why was the phone out while he was in the bathroom in the first place?

We argue over whose stuff is on whose side of the van. The Daughters really get a kick out of that one because they know I'm gonna win that one every time, much to Brian's dismay. Then we argue because Daughter 1 "coughed" her germs onto Daughter 2's side, so Daughter 2 blew her boogers onto Daughter 1's side. And it goes on like this for miles. I fashion a "pray for me" sign out of drive-thru napkins and wave them at passing truckers. Some of them honk and some of them indicate with their hands that praying is not what they have on their well-traveled and obviously desperate minds if they're signaling for me to do that.

Finally, we pull onto the gravel road that will lead two miles back to the farm where Brian grew up. It's quiet at this point, because The Daughters have decided that at this juncture in our travels, it would be a good time to settle in for a nap. They are out cold.

Seven hours and forty-four minutes later, we pull into the driveway. I tumble out of the van and kiss the ground, hoping there's no cow poop at that exact spot.

My father-in-law swings open his back door and says, "About time you got here!"

I challenge him to drive this family to the barn, which is approximately fifty yards away without making seventeen stops … I, of course, will be waiting in the house for their return, coloring a picture of Cinderella and using the bathroom whenever I want.

A Guaranteed Trip To Purgatory

It's not just long trips that make our family poster children for mental health institutions everywhere. Sometimes we can just drive fifteen minutes across town in an attempt to worship with our church family. Really, they are like a family. And I know they feel the same way about us as they often refer to us as the "children," this proves they love us as family.

I'm pretty sure that if Jesus had personally met the daughters during his short time here on this Earth, His quote would have been, "Suffer the little children to come unto me; but keep an eye on those daughters right there." Then he probably would have done the V with his fingers, pointing to His own eyes, then to The Daughters.

It's not that they're bad children. It's that they're irreverent children while in church (and anywhere else for that matter). Let's take this past Sunday for example.

First off, I'd love to take the blame for their craziness during church services, but our church provides donuts every Sunday morning. These donuts only serve to sugar up the kids; therefore, their wildness is absolutely no reflection on me. I think the other donut eaters are getting a little tired of my announcing that every single Sunday. But until I get off the hook for The Daughters' random acts of lunacy, I will be making that disclaimer from the pulpit every Sunday morning.

Brian has suggested that maybe if we fed them breakfast at home, they would be a bit more settled during the worship service. I have suggested to him that he's talkin' crazy talk. If we fed them at home, we'd have to get up at least five minutes earlier to unwrap the fiber bar and, really, I neither have that kind of time in my schedule nor that kind of energy in my body.

Can I get an Amen?

Actually, Brian and I try to be very proactive in our religious behaviors in order to have quiet and respectful church-daughters. On our way to church, we have conversations about being quiet and not talking when the pastor is talking; being respectful and keeping our heads bowed and our voices off during prayers. We will all stand when it's time to stand (not on the chairs) and sit when it's time to sit (not under the chairs). We won't play with the offering plate nor will we giggle if the word "ass" is said in scripture or hymn; this rule is mainly for Brian, but it bears repeating for all of us, right? [Note from my Editor: Giggle! You said "ass."] [Note from me to my Editor: I will snap my fingers at you, too.]

Daughter 1 and Daughter 2 serenely nod their heads and smile sweetly at us, murmuring "Yes, ma'am" and "Yes, sir."

This, my friends, is a guise. A devious little ruse they've perfected in an attempt to lure their momma into a false sense of sane behavior.

They are setting us up so that we can let our guards down. Because the minute "we are standing on holy ground" during the prelude, the circus that is Daughter 1 and Daughter 2 takes center ring.

This particular morning at church was no different, except that Brian was helping with the service so he was sitting on the other side of the sanctuary, probably laughing at me, but I can't be sure about that. The Daughters invited their friends to sit with them.

So, on this particular morning? I was single parenting it with two extra kids. And? It was noisy collection Sunday, which means that our Associate Pastor gave all the kids an old metal coffee can with which they were to collect special missions offering at the end of the service. Even empty, these cans are noisy. Especially noisy, as they are falling off the heads of children, causing said children to commence giggling when they should be praying. I'm just telling ya how it was. We don't have formal confession at our church, but I'm confessing it now.

Even after going to the bathroom after Sunday School (twice), The small-bladdered little blasphemers still have to go at least once during services. Daughter 2 quietly and sweetly asked me if she could go to the bathroom. I quietly and sweetly told her no. So she not-as-quietly and not-as-sweetly told me she was going to the bathroom. I gritted my teeth and told her noooo. And I shook my head violently to demonstrate what that word meant. I knew I had won this battle when she crossed her arms and sat back ... then she tooted. She farted in church like a frat boy.

I raised my eyes toward glory and silently mouthed, "Really??" And just for good measure, she tooted again. Then giggled. I took a deep breath in (big mistake after someone's just tooted next to you in church), gritted my teeth, grabbed her by the collar and loudly whispered, "Hurry." Every momma has a breaking point. Mary's was when Jesus stayed behind in the temple. Mine was when someone tooted in the temple.

If I didn't earn my spot in heaven this morning, I'm pretty sure I never will. Many people think that a little confession of one's sins is a deal-sealer. I'm here to tell you that for mommas, it's not confession. It's repression and possibly suppression. Either one really works.

If a momma can repress and suppress the urge to scream out, "FOR THE LOVE OF PETE, JUST QUIT IT!" during the worship service when a child has tapped the hymn book 4,938 times during the Gospel reading, then she's secured herself a very special place on high. If a momma can repress the urge to hiss, "Get your boogers out of your sister's face" during the Lord's Prayer, then she's going to eventually walk on streets of gold. If a momma can keep from giggling when Daughter 1 is quietly yanking hairs out of the boy in front of her, then through those ivory gates she shall pass. Okay—maybe I giggled just once, but it was funny, and right after the snort escaped my unwilling nose, I told her "don't." It still counts.

Finally, the benediction is said and we're all pledging that God will be with us 'til we meet again. I'm amazed at how the church clears. All of those people who, just an hour before, had commented on what a sweet family we were, are now sprinting out the door as I gathered shoes, purses, Bibles and Corn Nuts (yes, Corn Nuts) and attempted to leave God's house.

I know that when I find my place in glory, I'll have a mansion built especially for me. I just hope it comes with a nanny! And a housekeeper. Maybe a personal chef. Hopefully a masseuse, too.

Actual Questions The Daughters Have Asked During Church

Is it okay with God if we don't wear underwear to church?

How do you spell 'ransom'?

How does a woman get 'great with child'?

Is the Bible online?

Since I'm hungry now, can we just get up and walk out?

Why are you putting a check in there? When I asked if we could go to McDonalds, didn't you say we didn't have money for that? Was that a lie?

Geez, Momma—why didn't you shave your legs before coming to church?

If I promise to keep my pantyhose on, can I take off my shoes?

Can I go to the back row and practice my cartwheels?

Could I bring the DVD player next week if I watch *Evan Almighty*?

You just yawned; why can't I go to sleep?

What exactly happens if I don't tell God about cutting up all of Daughter 1's underwear?

Can I roll the dice on your phone if I promise not to yell 'crap'?

I'm so hungry—when's communion?

How can I love our neighbors if they stand in our yard and smoke?

Did that verse just say 'peace' or 'pizza'?

Will you scratch my back, then rub my shoulders and then massage my feet?

Can I call my friend and see what she's doing?

Do you have any scissors? What about a ruler? Do you have any matches? So what exactly do you even carry in your purse?

Daddy's checking his phone; why can't I just play one little game of poker on your phone?

Namaste Begins Closer To Noon

My lack of sleep, coupled with having to live with three crazies, really pushed me to a breaking point. Luckily, FloJo is an amazing yoga leader.

Over the course of this past year, FloJo has taken me under her wings and has taught me how to yoga … not to be confused with the time she taught me how to Dougie. [Note from my editor: Pause here to do a little dance. You know everyone is.] [Note from me: Pause granted.]

Pause.

Back to yoga.

Since I'm a good student, I'm pretty much an expert at yoga now.

Not really. But, I am pretty damned good.

Not really. But, I can do a spot-on sun salutation. Spot on, I tell ya.

Not really. But close enough.

And over the course of this past year, I have found that the sun salutation has served me well. I have discovered that when I'm tired or feeling low on energy, I can do (Perform? Act? Practice? I'll stick with "do") a few sun salutations and feel totally renewed. Well, not totally, but it does get me out of doing the immediate task at hand, so if nothing else, it's provided me with a new diversionary tactic for five to ten minutes or so to avoid the work that was making me so tired.

Yes, the sun salutation has served me well. And on this particular day, it served me on a silver platter. Let me explain.

I have been working an hour away from home for the past three weeks of my summer vacation. This means that not only do I have to get up in the morning (which I have avoided doing all summer); I have to get up early in the morning. Then, last week, Brian had an out-of-town training where he got to sleep in a bed with clean sheets and, I had to get up extra early to take The Daughters to my own momma's and then drive the hour to get to work.

Add to that horrific scenario that my supervisor expects me to begin actually working when I get there. Unfortunately, I'm not allowed to take my break first thing. Or second thing for that matter. I felt like I was working in some sweatshop sewing labels on sweatshirts that read "Kathie Lee."

Have I ever mentioned that I'm not a morning person? Well, I'm not. At all.

My friends, the combination of not sleeping well because Brian was away (you'd think with all that snoring absent from the night, I would sleep well) and having a couple of daughters who, at the age of four, began waking up several times a night after having slept through the night from the day they came screaming into the world (maybe it was me screaming) and having to wake up at an hour I had no idea existed until three weeks ago (who knew there were two five o'clocks in the day?) makes me one exhausted momma.

Today, I remembered what my FloJo, said about yoga: It'll give you energy and make you sweaty. And at

10:02 am this morning, I needed energy and I didn't care if I got any kind of sweaty. For the life of me, I couldn't figure out why I was seeing double and why my eyes kept closing of their own free will!

I took my break (it was a legitimate break time) and wandered between two tall library shelves just outside my workroom. I stretched my arms up high to begin my sun salutation and carefully swung them down to my toes. Slowly I stretched my feet out behind me and lowered myself into plank, a very wobbly and warped plank, but a plank nonetheless. Lowering myself even further, I became a stick and then stretched into upward facing dog. I heaved my tired self into downward facing dog, gathered my feet in and then stretched up and ended in mountain.

(Does anyone else giggle when they hear downward facing dog thinking of those silly moose in *Brother Bear*? No? Just me? Well, then.)

I took a deep breath in and began another salutation. This one, however, was more of a sunset benediction. I lowered into plank and then into stick and then I thought, "Hmmm. That carpet looks rough, but not THAT rough …" and then next thing I know, my stick was then more of a plucked dandelion.

And the carpet really wasn't that rough.

I'm not sure exactly how long I was napping on the floor, but I am thankful that my supervisor let the carpet imprint on my forehead and drool stain on my cheek be reprimand enough.

Tomorrow, instead of sun salutations, I'm going to try sangria with my breakfast. Wonder how my supervisor will feel about that?

Namaste, my friends!

The Other Side Of the Bed Gets a Lot Of Use

Brian and I are equal partners in our relationship. We always have been, and I foresee that we always will be. We have one checking account that we each share with equal responsibility. While I cook dinners, he's in charge of breakfast and lunch. Please don't say, "Wait, that's two meals!" Let me explain: by breakfast, I mean the unwrapping of a cereal bar. And by lunch I mean a yogurt, cheese stick and box of raisins tossed into a sack. If he has extra time, maybe he'll pour cereal into coffee mug. If you believe nothing else, I write, believe this: It's equal!

When The Daughters are sick, we take turns staying home with them. Brian puts them to bed and gets them up. I work the night hours. If he does the laundry, I put it away. If I load the dishwasher, he unloads it. We even take turns mowing the lawn. We both dust and vacuum and clean the toilets. We even share the backyard pool chores: He maintains it, and I use it.

Fair and equal distribution of all things within our marriage.

Okay. Fine. Let's revisit this on one tiny subject: the bed.

Don't worry! Keep reading! I'm not going all *Fifty Shades* here. That'll be the next book.

See, Brian and I do equally split the bed. We each have our sides. I'm just not certain it's as fair as Brian thinks it is.

See, Brian's half is the top half. Half? Who am I kidding? Brian's side is the top of the mattress.

The early years of our marriage, this was perfectly acceptable because I'd snuggle right up with him and lay in the crook of his shoulder. It was quaint. It was cute. Our friends who had been married longer than we had complained and moaned about their partners not sharing the bed. Brian and I scoffed at them. We'd never be that way.

I'm not sure when I began to think twice about my part of the bed being the sides that I clung to every night. I think it might have been sometime around my thirty-eighth week of pregnancy with Daughter 1, when a little nudge from a sleeping Dad sent me and my grossly obtuse belly right over the edge—figuratively and literally. Brian wrote off my swift kick to his backside to pregnancy hormones.

By the time Daughter 2 was on her way and Daughter 1 had taken to sleep walking right into our bed, we made a joint decision to get a king-sized bed. And by joint decision, I mean that Brian agreed with me after yet another pregnancy-hormone-induced swift kick to his baby-makin' equipment.

It was heaven. Right up to the point when Brian claimed the top half as his own. I realized this was a bigger problem than I cared to admit when I woke up with my head on the nightstand, using the lamp as my pillow.

"Something's got to give! You have to stop pushing me out of bed!" I shouted early one morning. At three o'clock.

Brian snored. Nothing wakes him up.

When we had a more rational and aware conversation the next morning, Brian had a quick solution. "Just wake me up."

This, my friends, is one of the many reasons I love him. What a crack up! He just makes me laugh. So witty and funny and full of jokes! Of course, he had no idea why I was laughing. I reminded him that once, early in our marriage, a drug bust occurred on our front lawn—complete with a high speed chase and eight law enforcement vehicles with lights, sirens and bullhorns. He slept through the whole thing. Including my play-by-play commentary, nudging, slapping and poking!

When faced with this accurate and damning information, he offered another solution: when he pushed me off of one side, I should just get up and go around to the other side. It wasn't ideal, but I was willing to try just about anything to get more than an hour's worth of sleep at a time.

The next night, I had been asleep about an hour when I felt the first nudge. I got up and went to his side of the bed.

An hour later … another nudge. Again, I switched sides.

An hour later … another nudge. I noisily switched sides.

An hour later … another nudge. I got up and watched DVR'd episodes of Dr. Oz in which he told me I needed more sleep than was physically possible in my home.

That night, I didn't get any sleep, but I did lose three pounds from all the walking between sides. Still: Not my idea of a good night's sleep.

The next night, I decided to fight back. He nudged. I nudged. He nudged. I nudged harder. He nudged and I point-blank punched! He thought it was foreplay and began whispering sweet nothings in his sleep. Dream on, Mister, dream on!

The next night, I had it all figured out. Before I went to sleep, I wrapped myself in the sheets and comforter and then tucked it under the mattress. I was going nowhere that night.

And, truth is I didn't go far. The good news is that the wrap-and-tuck acts as a hammock off the side of the bed, and while it's not ideal, I like to pretend I'm on a tropical island, lounging in the rope-braids of a hammock hung between two palm trees.

Hey. A girl can dream … just not on the bed.

Date Night? That's A Matter Of Opinion

I'm pretty sure that going out to eat with The Daughters causes just as much trial and tribulation as Glenn Beck at an Occupy San Francisco event. When we go out to eat as a family, Brian and I typically give The Daughters a few choices as to where they would like to go. This, my friends, is mistake number one. All the parenting experts will tell you that giving children choices and allowing them to make family decisions will lead to responsible, confident adults.

Like the card game of yore: I cry bullshit!

Who are these parenting experts and why didn't they have children of their own to try these theories out in real world situations? I'm telling you right now that if Dr. Spock had children of his own (or did he?), he'd have said, "Choices, Schmoices! Lay down the law and stick to it. Save yourself the heart ache, Captain Kirk."

Or was that the wrong Spock?

Clearly it's not a matter of what we want to eat, but how we want to be entertained while we wait for our potato skins and chicken fingers. When we decide that we'll go out to eat, we'll all get in the minivan and say something along the lines of this: "Daughters, you get to choose: do you want to go to the BBQ place that has the buffalo coloring sheets or the singing place that has the color-on table covers or the place out in the mall that has the high chairs but only gives you two crayons?"

Brian and I would be happy to go to any of these places. The Daughters would also be just as happy to eat at any of these places, but why take the easy route when a full-blown sibling fight would suck so much more of our energy!?

Daughter 1, the artist, wants to go to the BBQ place because she's creating a collection of colored buffalos, and she's really excited to add a monochromatic buffalo to her collection (which is stashed, by the way, on the floor of the back seat of Brian's SUV). Daughter 2, ever the baby however, refuses to go to the BBQ place because one time when she was three, we joked that she'd have to stay there and wash dishes and the server said he'd gladly take the help and that just freaked her out, and she's never going there again as long as she lives. Her choice is the place at the mall because she likes to feel tall when she sits on the stools. But, Daughter 1 will never go there because they only give you two crayons and she obviously needs more crayons than just two since she's a serious artist. At this point, I remind her that I carry, in my way-too-heavy purse, two complete boxes of crayons. To which she replies, "But, Momma, I don't want to stress you out by having you dig in your purse and get the crayons out just for me!" Oh, sure … don't stress me out over crayons; that's certainly my biggest stressor.

Eventually, Brian just gets in his car and starts the engine and we end somewhere entirely different (where he wanted to go all along, truth be told) and not one person in our family is happy with the selection, except Brian who's happily munching on cornmeal-battered catfish and tuning us all out.

Luckily, Brian and I actually do hire a babysitter at least once a month, or we pawn The Daughters off on Nana if she's feeling forgetful and doesn't remember the circus that was her house the last time she kept them. Our dates are generally nothing extravagant because our babysitter and Nana have our phone numbers and use them frequently, so we go out to eat and then do something local and quick. Just last weekend, for example, we went to the local catfish place; I'll give you three guesses as to who picked that one. After dinner, Brian asked what I wanted to do next.

Well, I had a few things I wanted to get at Hellmart, so we could start there. And since we were already there, we might as well get our groceries for the week. And stock up on toilet paper. Then, by the time we got through the 32-person long line, it was time to head home.

On the way home, Brian let out a big, man-sized sigh. "Hardly seems worth paying a babysitter for!"

"What does?"

"Just going out to eat and to Hellmart. Not much of a date night."

I placed my hand on his thigh and spoke slowly and lowly, "Oh, honey, eating dinner without an argument and shopping Hellmart without chasing kids or carts? Well-worth the money we pay a babysitter! In fact, I'm so relaxed after this trip to Hellmart, that I can guarantee you're going to be one happy man tonight!"

"Guaranteed?"

"Well," I said while looking at him with bedroom eyes, "If you unload all the groceries."

Momma gets her money's worth out of the babysitter.

Hellmart Drives Me Crazy —Or Maybe I Was Already There?

My task is usually simple: grab the things on my list, nothing more and nothing less, and go home. I come prepared. List? Check. Earth-friendly bags? Check. Coupons? Check. The Daughters? Check. It's pretty straight forward, week after week. Bread, milk, eggs, applesauce, fruit, veggies, toilet paper. Ya know, the staples. I am ready to make my way into Hellmart. This, my friends, is where it gets fuzzy in my mind.

Somehow, my list of twenty items becomes a cartful of stuff we don't need. Paper plates shaped like elephants, Barbie vitamins, and about twenty-two Weight Watchers meals because there's never a better time to start a diet than after you've just grabbed five brownie mixes because they're on sale. I also grab twenty pounds of potatoes because I think I bought some potatoes last week, but I don't remember if it was last week or the week before and did we have potato soup last week or this week? And now we're buying a real pineapple. These things are NOT on my list.

Three hours later, I leave Hellmart with The Daughters, all my coupons (because I didn't remember to tell the checker in time that I even had them), twenty-two extra plastic sacks (because the earth friendly bags were under the dog food) and $200 less in my checking account. How does this happen? What happens to my brain that I, an educated momma, can't seem to stay on target when I enter Hellmart with The Daughters? Where's the milk? I did grab the milk, right?

And … Hey! Who moved the van? Did I even drive the van? Thank heavens for panic buttons or we'd still be wandering the parking lot. I will be beyond glad when I can just make a list, send The Daughters and sit at home eating bonbons. But, I'm not sure when that day will come (if ever). My usually brilliantly smart daughters, more times than not, lack basic common sense. They get it their lack of common sense from Brian.

Typically, when I have to go to Hellmart for any reason, I kick and scream and throw a fit and beg Brian to just hire someone to go get our weekly allotment of bread and toilet paper because I simply cannot stand to go. Something happens to people when they walk into Hellmart: They become rude, self-absorbed, angry and bitter. And, yes, I include myself in that statement. Add to that attitude two Daughters who want and need everything, driving their momma to the point of crackin' open a wine cooler right there on aisle fourteen. It's just not a pleasant experience. Well, the wine cooler's alright. [Note from my editor: Makes you wish they'd change those Bible Belt liquor laws, doesn't it?] [Note from me: Damn straight.]

After much tears and threats of no ugly bumpin' until his uglies are shriveled up, Brian offered this suggestion: He'd go to Hellmart and do the shopping for us.

"Great! Then I get to stay home and relax alone."

"You mean relax at home with The Daughters?" he questioned, clearly forgetting that his chance at a lifetime of lucky was on the line. "Relax" and "The Daughters" never fit into the same sentence without a sense of hilarity or utter fiction sneaking in.

Well, what a silly man. If I didn't have to take The Daughters with me, it might not be nearly as bad as I'd made it out. So, I offered him the choice: I go to Hellmart BY. MY. SELF. Or he could go with The Daughters. Or he could make friends with the brothers down at the Perpetually Celibate monastery.

Thus began my weekly trip to Hellmart—alone. This clearly worked out much better. We saved money by not buying the 42-pack of cinnamon gum (which no one in our house chews) and I saved a very little bit of my sanity. I only have a very little bit left, so I'll take what I can get.

Last week, however, we found ourselves in need of groceries (these dad-gummed Daughters think they need to eat), and Brian and Daughter 1 were at softball practice. That left me with the very awkward dilemma: Do I go to Hellmart with Daughter 2? Do I put off going to Hellmart until Brian and Daughter 1 get home? OR, do I lock Daughter 2 in her room and pray no one comes looking for her and just go alone? After the little sneak picked her way out of her bedroom and beat me to the van, I opted to take her with me. She's so quick in so many ways.

I decided from the start that I would lay down the ground rules and be firm. I would be strong and in control of my grocery buying.

After putting my foot down before we even left the driveway, Daughter 2 asked, "Does this mean I can't ask for just candy or anything else? What if it's healthy? Can we get something I want if it has a coupon on it? How about you buy a grape soda for yourself and then share all of it with me?" By the time we actually got to Hellmart, I had told Daughter 2 "No" approximately 32,908 times. As we walked into the store, and I grabbed the cart, Daughter 2 asked one last question, "Can I drive the cart?" What the hell? It was a question I could say yes to.

Until she hit the back of my heels. Then she knocked over the shampoo display. Then she hit the back of someone else's heels. Then she rammed head on into someone else's cart. Finally, for the safety and sanity of all who were in Hellmart on that Sunday afternoon, I took over the cart.

"Uhhhhhhh! Momma! You said I could drive it!" she quickly complained. And I quickly ignored the old man who shook a fist in our direction and his wife whose arthritic hands were still capable of extending just one finger. I promised Daughter 2 that she could push the cart out to the van when we were finished. What harm could there be in that, right? Not many people around and we parked close.

So after checking out, with only one thing that was not on my list (I have no idea who those Cool Mint Oreo cookies are for), I let Daughter 2 navigate her way to the van. Right as we walked out of the door, I dropped my sunglasses. Daughter 2 went on; she had one foot on the cart and one foot was propelling her forward as if on a skateboard. Then she saw a penny on the ground and hopped off the cart to retrieve it because it was head side up and that meant that she could keep it and have good luck!

I stood up from picking up my sunglasses just in time to see the cart sail down the parking aisle. I sprinted as much as any "Couch to 5K" week-two dropout can sprint toward the cart, which just kept sailing away. As I passed the hundreds of cars, I couldn't help but notice just how many Mercedes and Jaguars were in the lot. Who knew the rich and famous did their biddin' at Hellmart? Then I silently, but sincerely, thanked God almighty that the cart went straight down the open aisle and not straight into their shiny paint jobs.

I just knew that the little dip in the parking lot would surely slow down the cart, but I swear to you right now, that cart caught air. I thought about just stopping and letting the groceries go, then I remembered my Cool Mint Oreos, and I caught my second wind. Daughter 2, ever the competitive child, passed me by and I was ever so grateful that she had found her a lucky penny and was now going to save the cart, which was, oddly, going in a completely straight line. Daughter 2 came upon the cart and she passed it. And the cart just kept going. And going. And going. Daughter 2 reached the end of the parking lot and turned around, her little fists in the air pumping as if she were a Guidette at the Jersey Shore. Thankfully, the cart came to rest just beside Daughter 2, barely bumping the curb as if it were truly mourning its loss to such a great runner as Daughter 2. I slowed my pace a little and not just because the old couple from the produce aisle backed out right on my heels. I slowed more because my ears were pounding louder than a banger's low-rider on a Friday night in downtown LA.

I met up with the cart and Daughter 2, both of whom I was now convinced were out to give me a heart attack. I turned the cart around and told Daughter 2 to push the cart, without letting go, back to the van.

"Nah," she commented as she walked away. "I'm kind of tired of pushing it. You can push it now." And she skipped back up to the front of the store, where our van was waiting for us, just three cars away from the front doors. So, I did what any other out-of-shape, family-lovin' momma would do: I sat down and opened the Oreos. I ate a few and then, leaving the cart behind, I walked back to the van, sans cart.

Sure, driving the van down to the cart probably wasted gas, but my family needed groceries and I was sure I didn't have it in me to push the cart and walk all the way back to the van. When Brian complained about the five broken eggs and the smashed loaf of bread, I reminded him he was lucky that he had more to eat than Cool Mint Oreos. Ultimately, though, he is completely to blame: if he would just take us out to eat for every single meal, I wouldn't have to buy groceries and the kitchen would stay clean. Complain about that, Mister.

Momma vs. The Coppers — They'll Never Take Me Alive!

I would like to thank the kindly police officer who, in his singular act of protecting and serving, mentally upset my children (and their momma) for life.

That's right, my friends. This week as The Daughters and I were heading home from school, the unthinkable happened: I was pulled over by an officer of the law.

We were in a construction zone, so when I saw the lights appear in my rearview mirror, I said the prayer of drivers everywhere who are subjected to rear-sighted blue and red lights, "Please let him pass me."

I pulled over and I'll be damned if the cop car didn't pull over as well. Dammit. Daughter 1, my ever-worrying child, immediately questioned why we were pulling over. Daughter 2, my ever-clueless child wanted to go to Sonic and get a cherry slushy. "No, a green apple slushy. No, cherry. Wait! Grape!"

I rolled down my window and waited for him to tell me that he had pulled me over just because he so admired my righteous driving skills with two kids in the van on a Monday afternoon. Remember when they used to pull people over just to tell them they did a good job? Didn't they? I swear that's what my dad told me when I was 7 years old and he got pulled over.

Daughter 1 quickly figured out that there was indeed a policeman approaching the van and immediately she launched into full-blown worry mode.

"Momma! He's going to arrest you! Isn't he? You're going to be arrested! Will we have to go to foster care? Will I have to stay with the van until Daddy can bail you out? Will you be a fugitive of the week? I can't believe you're going to be arrested! I am so embarrassed, Momma!"

I snapped my fingers at her and told her to get it together. I hissed at her, "You calm yourself down and let me do the talking. I won't go to the pokey because you can't get it together!" Then I snapped my fingers again. Just because it sounded authoritative.

She grabbed my phone and immediately began recording. She winked as my phone beeped. "I got your back, Momma," she mouthed.

Daughter 2 asked again for a slushy, this time orange. Then the officer was at the window.

I should have let either one of them do the talking.

The following is the actual conversation as transcribed from the video Daughter 1 took using my phone "to use in a court of law, Momma!"

Officer: Do you know why I stopped you?

Me: Um … speeding in a construction zone?

Silent voice in my head: What? Don't give him any ideas!

Officer: No.

Me: General speeding?

Silent voice in my head: SHUT UP! Do not admit to anything! This isn't a guessing game!

Officer: Uhhh—I don't think so.

Me: Running the stop sign?

Silent voice in my head: You are going to jail. Daughter 1 was right!

Officer: Did you?

Me: I don't think so.

Officer: You don't think so?

Me: Umm … Pretty sure I didn't?

Silent voice in my head: Go ahead and admit to inattentive driving! You're certainly not paying any attention to me!

Officer: Actually [pointing back to the rear of the van] …

Me: [totally interrupting him] My tail light's out. Figures. It's all my husband's fault. He's the one you're after. Not me. He maintains the vehicles and I maintain the house. We're a very traditional, normally law-abiding family!

Silent voice in my head: Just keep talking. You're made of money, right?

Officer: Well, let me check. Step on your brakes and let me check.

[Steps to back of the van; returns to blabbering idiot in the driver's seat]

Officer: No. Brake lights work. Let me just tell you why I pulled you over, OK? Your tag has expired.

Me: [Feeling extreme relief] Oh. No. I renewed it.

Silent voice in my head: You did do that, right? Didn't you?

Officer: The tag has expired. By four months, ma'am.

Me: Well, I paid it.

Officer: Doesn't appear that you have. May I see your insurance?

Me: Sure. [shakily handing insurance to him]

Officer: This is expired.

Me: WHAT? Are you sure? I paid that, too. Look again.

Silent voice in my head: See you in eight to ten, if you have good behavior.

Long story short: I found the correct insurance verification (up-to-date and everything); I renewed my tag at the tag office when I discovered that I, indeed, had not renewed it as I thought I had; Daughter 1 finished her video of my defense and didn't appear to suffer any long-term effects of her hyperventilation; and Daughter 2 asked the officer to please arrest me as I told her she was not getting a slushy since I had to go speedy-quick to the tag agency.

Actual Conversation Between A Manager At The "Local Fresh Market" And An Elderly Customer The Day Before Thanksgiving, Overheard As I Was Standing In Line To Buy French Vanilla Ice Cream For My Father-In-Law To Eat With His Pecan Pie. As Far As I Know, The Ice Cream Is Still In The Freezer, But The Conversation I Overheard Will Live In My Memory Infinitely.

Customer: I'm looking for your real eggs.

Manager: The brown eggs are on the back wall.

Customer: No, I want the real ones. The white ones.

Manager: The white ones will be on the truck that will arrive at five o'clock tonight. But they aren't real.

Customer: Oh yes they are. I can't stand those brown ones.

Manager: The brown ones come from chickens. They are the only real ones.

Customer: Where do the white ones come from?

Manager: The plant. That's why they have all the cholesterol in them. They are manufactured.

Customer: That's ridiculous.

Manager: No. It's the truth. There are egg plants all over this country that manufacture eggs.

Customer: Well, I don't care. I'll come back later for my real eggs.

Manager: Suit yourself. You'll only be killing your own body.

Customer: And my family! The eggs are for breakfast.

Momma VS The Empty Roll

Raise your hands if you (The Momma) are the only one in your house qualified and able to change a roll of toilet paper? I thought so. Girls, it's time that we unite!

I have no idea how it happens. I have no idea why it happens. But, this I swear to you: it does happen every single time I go to the bathroom in our house, and we have three toilets, I am always left stranded. If I'm not stranded, then I'm left with false hope—which may be worse.

You know false hope, right? It's where it looks like there's toilet paper on the roll, but really, it's just two and a half squares wrapped around the tube. Just enough to make you feel safe enough to go ahead and unzip but it's not enough to really do much with, unless you just have a runny nose-and even then, it's barely sufficient.

Brian is an educated man. He has a masters degree, and he earned it before the Internet really took hold, so it's gotta be legitimate, right? He has worked in the financial world and in the educational world. That right there is enough, my friends, to make my brain spin. He can kill spiders and chlorinate a pool. He can change oil and birth a calf. He can assemble a bicycle he bought off eBay with instructions that were written by kindergarten students in a Central Asian country school. He can wake up without an alarm and can text, talk and type at the same time. Changing the toilet paper roll? That's a mystery to this man.

The Daughters are smart cookies. Daughter 1 reads two grade levels above her class. Daughter 2 can tell jokes—funny jokes, not just funny to a preschool student, but funny to people who aren't even related to her. They both potty trained early and easily. They both take instruction well from teachers and from coaches and from Girl Scout leaders. The empty toilet roll? It baffles them.

Please understand that it's not that I'm frantic about toilet paper. Okay. It is that I'm frantic about toilet paper. I'm desperately frantic about toilet paper. I'm borderline obsessively-frantic about toilet paper. I scour the weekly ads to see who has the best deals and then I buy toilet paper from all of them. My deepest fear is something happening to my family. My second deepest fear is running out of toilet paper.

I prefer to have no less than four rolls of toilet paper stashed in the cabinet behind each toilet. I have at least two twelve-double-roll packs of toilet paper in the hall closet at all times. If the world of Hellmart should come to an end and there'd be no place to get toilet paper anymore, I'm prepared. Forget drinking water! Forget canned foods. Forget matches and batteries and lights! I've got my Cottonelle, and all is well with the world.

So where does it go in my house when I need it most? I have no idea. It just ceases to be.

Inevitably, as soon as I take my seat, I discover no toilet paper. I maneuver around to the cabinet behind me without compromising myself too much in my untissued state. The toilet paper is gone. Just gone. Clearly, we're not taking toilet paper preparation serious enough in *mi casa*. I have no idea where I have failed as a homemaker. Okay, I have lots of ideas where I have failed.

I holler to The Daughters to come and help me out by bringing dear ol' Mom, "the one who birthed ya," some toilet paper. Daughter 2, who clearly has a soft spot in her heart for me, will show up with four squares from another bathroom, smile sweetly and skip away. I holler for Daughter 1. She's a bit more advanced. She acts 13 and huffs and sighs and rolls her eyes even though she's only 8; eventually, she rescues me with a roll of toilet paper she belabored from the hall closet. "Duh."

I explained to Brian that we undoubtedly have a problem. "No one seems to remember to replace the toilet paper but me!" I whined.

He assures me that it's not true. There was that one time when his parents were coming for a visit, "Remember, before we had kids?" He did, indeed, make sure the toilets had a whole roll of toilet paper handy. "That one time. Remember?" Oh, he'll be remembering that "one time," all right. I hope that "one time" memory keeps him warm on some cold winter night.

In my efforts to raise more prepared children, I had a heart-to-heart with The Daughters. "It's not fun to be left without toilet paper when you've gone to the bathroom."

Daughter 1 brags that she's never been left without toilet paper; sometimes she does use a lot because she likes to be extra clean. Daughter 2 declares that she doesn't even use the stuff; it takes too much time away from Barbie. So she's not the one leaving me high and not dry.

"Please," I beg the whole family that evening as I'm dragging in my buy-one-get-one 24-roll purchases

"Please, please, please—if you find the toilet roll empty and there's no more toilet paper in the bathroom—please replace it."

They all promise that if it ever happens to them, they'll quickly appease my toilet paper mania by keeping the bathroom well stocked. But, they all swear, it never runs out when they are in there … uh-huh.

I cock my head to the side, "So you're telling me that you've never been in the bathroom when the toilet paper has run out?

"That's right!"

"You got it!"

"I don't even use it!"

"Then maybe someone comes in, walks past the computer, the DVR, the digital camera, the TV, the gaming system, the karaoke machine and takes our toilet paper. Just our toilet paper?"

Brian looks deep into my eyes and lovingly says, "Maybe." Well, maybe just this one time, he'll get to experience sleeping outside with no toilet paper. Not that it'd even make him any difference.

Define "Alone Time"

My morning routine works so well for me because it's a time when I am alone. I am naked, in the bathroom, behind closed doors, alone. And, as all the mommas out there can attest to, that almost never happens. Most certainly, any other given time of day when I find myself in the bathroom either to take care of my bidness or for any other reason out there, I can assure you I won't be alone. And if I am alone, it won't be for long.

I have decided that the person who invented the bathroom door was a dad. And I'll tell you why it was a dad: a momma would have never wasted her time on such a useless object.

Out of a weird sense of self-torture, I counted the number of times this week that I actually got to go to the bathroom all by myself in my own house. It took some crazy accounting skills to get this tallied up, but I did it. Over the course of this week, I have actually gone to the bathroom all by myself twice.

Two times.

More than once, but less than three times.

One of those times was at four in the morning, but it still counted.

It's the truth, my friends. Mommas have no right to expect privacy while taking care of bathroom business.

The Daughters could be outside and down the street pestering the neighbors about their motorcycles and no sooner would I gently close the door and take my seat then BAM! The door would fly open and I'd be refereeing a fight over whose MP3 player has the cooler music on it!

And since Daughter 1 opted to have the Black Eyed Peas on her player and Daughter 2 didn't like black eyed peas, the vegetable, clearly Daughter 1 has the cooler MP3. Am I right or am I right?

Despite the swiftness in which I was able to complete my required momma-judgment, The Daughters remained at my knees discussing Easter shoes, dinner plans, sleepovers and why schools should allow pajama day every day.

I know what you are thinking: what momma doesn't want her offspring to gather at her knee soaking in all the maternal goodness the momma has to offer.

Answer? Me. At least I don't need their soaking (draining?) presence while I'm on the throne.

Listen to their excuses for barging in on my toitie time and tell me if you believe any of them were necessary for that exact moment:

"Momma! Are you planning on fixing broccoli for dinner? Because I am not eating it if you are fixing it."

"Momma! If we act right now, we can get two pillow pals for the price of one plus shipping and handling, but you have to act—right now!"

"Momma! Daughter 2 moved your 'spring' sign around and now it says 'spirng'!"

"Momma! Is it alright if I eat the rest of the Thin Mint cookies? Because I just did."

"Honey! You won't believe what this guy just did on TV! He knocked ten plates out from underneath ten eggs and didn't break any!"

Yes. You heard correctly. Even Brian barges in on my tee-tee time.

Toward the end of this week, as I started growing weary of my little accounting experiment and longed for the privacy only a stinky port-a-potty could afford me, I began to carefully calculate answering nature's call.

One desperate evening, I had *Wizards of Waverly Place* on the TV, freshly-baked chocolate chip cookies on the kitchen counter. I had Fergie and Will.i.am telling them what a good night tonight would be in the bedroom. Ummm. (Wait. I had the song blaring in their bedroom. There was going to be no good night in their bedroom.) I even let Bo, the dumb dog in the house. If he couldn't wreck havoc and provide a diversion, I didn't know who could. As an added bonus: Brian was watching old reruns of *Dougie Howser, MD* on Hulu on the laptop.

Clearly, this was my moment for some alone time to let my body do what comes most naturally.

I tiptoed into the bathroom, silently closed the door-and locked it!—and I sat down to do my business. Ahhhh … heaven. Solitude! Finally, I could hear myself tinkle.

I picked up the latest copy of Martha Stewart's Unnatural Living (that I may or may not have smuggled out of the doctor's office, because I am totally too cheap to pay that much for a magazine) and relaxed to do my business and day dream about the ways I could use dried rose buds and old bed sheets to create a bed-and-breakfast feel right in my very own bedroom. Yeah, that'll happen.

I finished my magazine and my bid-ness and reached for the toilet paper.

What I found was an empty roll. So, I hollered for someone to bring me some toitie paper.

No response. Oh shit. Pun intended.

I yelled and banged on the wall.

Nothing.

Finally, after another flip-through of Martha's suggestions for a smooth-running home including details on how to knit a toilet paper holder for every bathroom in your home, Brian timidly knocks on the door asking if I'm okay.

Not that he was concerned all that much. It was just that if I was planning on fixing mushrooms for dinner, he was not going to eat them.

Things I Have Done In The Bathroom, While Sitting On The Toilet

(That Will Not Gross You Out ... Too Much)

- ✓ Signed field trip permission slips
- ✓ Read Dr. Seuss books
- ✓ Opened a can of chicken noodle soup
- ✓ Poured root beer from a two-liter bottle into a small juice cup with a lid and a straw
- ✓ Braided hair (not my own)
- ✓ Braided hair (my own)
- ✓ Arranged a play date for that exact moment with the neighbor kids
- ✓ Put on and tied roller blades
- ✓ Bandaged a scrape on the knee from above-mentioned roller blades
- ✓ Applied Frankenstein make-up
- ✓ Painted toenails (not my own)
- ✓ Removed toenail polish (not my own)
- ✓ Tasted a new nacho recipe Daughter 1 created—using dog food (I didn't know that part until it was in my mouth)
- ✓ Helped write a report about the state of Delaware, or "The First State" as we experts like to call it
- ✓ Took a political survey over the phone (actually, that was kind of appropriate, eh?)
- ✓ Texted Brian for more toilet paper

Oh, Yes, She Did: My Very Own Momma Bought Me a Swimsuit

It was swimsuit season, and I was still trying to reach my goal of looking like Heidi Klum. I hadn't gone swimsuit shopping. My adoring and helpful mom, who does not swim, has been swimsuit shopping. And she bought me a swimsuit.

Go ahead. Read that again. My mother bought me a swimsuit. Me, her over-40 year old daughter. Received a swimsuit. From my own momma.

I tossed the sack aside, gagged on the words, "Gee you shouldn't have." I didn't even look in the sack, that's just how grateful I was.

"Go try it on," she prodded. I mumbled that I would do it later.

"Oh, go do it now," she insisted. I told her I had to feed the baby.

"Please just go put it on so I can see it," she said yanking the bag of cheese balls out of my hands and pulling my 6-year-old baby onto her lap. Then she added, "I want to see it before I'm called from this earthly home," and turned her mouth downward.

Momma guilt won. Kinda. I grabbed the swimsuit sack and headed to the bedroom. I tossed it in the corner, lay across my bed and checked my email on my phone for about ten minutes. I emerged from my bedroom, pronounced it "cute," said my thanks and snatched my cheese balls back.

There was no point in my even trying it on. I knew with every fashion fiber in my Faded Glory body that I would not like whatever it was my own momma had picked out for me. Ever since I was 6 years old and wanted to wear my way cute Wonder Woman Underoos on the outside of my shorts and my mom said, "No way, Jose," we have just not seen eye to eye on fashion.

Okay, confession time: The Underoos belonged to my younger sister; I didn't actually have any Underoos of my own. But still, you can clearly see how that woman tried to dominate my fashion sense even at an early and tender age, right?

It's not that my momma looks bad and has no taste. It's that her taste is very much different from my taste. Let me put it this way: My taste is like a fine wine—something to be savored and enjoyed and is appreciated by all. Her taste is like Pepto Bismol—it's tolerable when you need it, but in the end, it'll gag ya. I'm sure she sees our differences the same way. [Note from my editor: Same with my mom and me.] [Note from me: I'm sure our daughters won't feel the same way since we're so much cooler than our moms.]

So basically, we respect each other's fashion sense and don't mention it otherwise. Well, except when I'm wearing a dress. And I only wear a dress on three occasions: A funeral, a wedding or to church (on the rare occasion that I wake up earlier than my alarm). And on those few-and-far-between occasions, we will talk fashion. Unfortunately, that conversation includes the terms "18-hour" and "Playtex" way more than I would ever want them to.

And that brings us up to this weekend. We had friends over to swim and my swimsuits were either dirty or they had shrunk over the winter (weird, huh?). So, I grabbed the bag my mom had given me. At the very least, I could toss my cover-up over it or stand around with a towel wrapped around me.

I carefully opened the bag and pulled out a suit that obviously, my mom had picked up by mistake because it was cute. I put it on and walked out to the pool. The Daughters said, "Momma! We want a suit like that!" Brian looked at me and said, "So you found a suit you liked, did ya?"

I glanced sideways at him, "Do you like it?"

Brian looked me up and down and sized me up, "Yes, I do like it. You could enter a pageant with that suit." Before you start sighing and saying things like, "How sweet," just know that he had a poker game that night and needed me to help him set it up and make jalapeño-infused chocolate-chocolate cake. Also, he's a smart man. Plus he doesn't really like sleeping on the recliner.

Amazingly, we all agreed that this suit was indeed styling, even if it did come from my own momma.

And cute or not, I'm not sure how I feel about it: wearing a swimsuit that my mom picked out does, indeed, make me feel like I'm pageant ready. Look out, Miss Shady Lodge for Seniors: there may be new blood in this year's contest.

The Fashion Police — I Never Saw 'Em Coming

As a young, single professional, I wanted to look the part, so I shopped. Wait. I didn't just shop; I shopped hard. I hit high-end department stores and didn't wait for the sales. I bought outfits that looked good and screamed, "Professional!" in every color. When I'd get my paycheck, I'd quickly go charge a new outfit or four. Yes, I said *charge*. I'm a teacher, for heaven's sake. I had to use my paycheck for things like rent and groceries and that pesky luxury called electricity. Forgive me, Dave Ramsey, for I have charged.

I had a closet full of professional clothes. I wore a different power outfit every day. I thought I was setting a fine example for my young and impressionable students in that when you dressed the part, you looked the part and when you looked the part then people believed that you knew what you were doing. (Yes, I taught English; please do not dissect that sentence!) [Note from my editor: I will not dissect that sentence because you asked me nicely and because I wouldn't even know where to start.]

I also taught middle school, so unless I looked like Christina Aguilera (which I didn't), they wouldn't have noticed what I was wearing even if my clothes were on fire (which they were, but only once).

The funny thing was this: I lived for Fridays. Fridays were jean days. As much as I loved my professional wardrobe, I loved dressing down even more.

Eventually, I changed schools and had a principal who was a bit more contemporary. In my classes, we would read on the floor; and, when we would sit comfy on the floor propped up by massive pillows and beanbags, I would have to wear jeans so as to not ruin my professional attire. Then we began writing while lounging on the floor, surrounded by pillows and lap desks and fun-colored pens, and I would have to wear jeans so I could be on the floor with them and assist them and guide them on their learning journeys. And eventually I earned tenure and wore jeans every day no matter what we were doing. Because that, my friends, may be the best part about having tenure: wearing jeans every day.

My closet was still full of professional-looking clothes that stayed packed away in my walk-in closet. Never to be touched again, until Brian moved in and demanded a few hangers of his own. What a diva.

I got rid of a few outfits when The Daughters came along and ruined anything nice I had left with their throw up, play dough and so-called washable markers. Finally, I embraced the fact that I am not a fancy-schmancy dresser. I am blue jeans queen all the way, baby! Neil Diamond became my soul mate and I believed he was singing to me when he said, "I like to say, we'll do okay, forever in blue jeans." And—my friends—most days, "okay" is a grand goal.

Of course, there are still many occasions for which I do have to dress up: church (only on Easter and Christmas when people who haven't seen me since the last Easter or Christmas were likely to come to church with the sole intent being to judge my attire), Brian's work parties (during which I turn into a 15-year-old girl and must get approval of my outfit from every person I know), weddings and funerals.

Weddings and funerals, for me, are easy to dress for. I saved one dress from my dress-professional days that works for both and has for about seven years now. If it's a funeral, I'll wear pearl earrings, the gemstone of respect, right? If it's a wedding, I'll wear amethyst earrings; it is a party after all.

I have bought two new wedding-appropriate dresses (they aren't really wedding dresses, per se) in the past four years. I bought a coral linen dress for my sister-in-law's outdoor summer wedding and a blue linen dress for my sister's outdoor fall wedding. Did you know that coral fabric will attract the mosquitoes? I haven't confirmed this on Google, of course; all my data is qualitative (and in scar-form up and down my arms). Since both dresses are linen and both dresses require that I iron them or take them to the cleaners, they are really not practical as my wedding or funeral dress. Therefore, they hang in the closet. Wrinkled. I think I have cleaned them. [Note from my editor: Never buy linen! That shit is way too wrinkly unless you plan to just stand and never move. But, your dresses sound pretty.] [Note from me: I hear ya on the wrinkly shit, sister.]

My church attire consists of slacks. God bless the woman who said, "I ain't wearing a dress no more!" I don't do dresses too much in church. For one, I sometimes volunteer in the nursery (if for no other reason than to not wear a dress to church) and dresses and nursery kids usually equal embarrassment on my part when that which is under my dress is exposed by a clingy toddler or I am inadvertently groped by an emergent walker who is grasping for anything, namely my undies, to pull up with. And second, we generally run "late" to church; late in my wardrobe means a run in my pantyhose. [Note to my readers: I originally had "runny pantyhose" and my editor said it sounded gross, which I thought was funny, so I decided to share than phrase with you anyway.] [Note from my editor: LOL!]

I do get all dolled up for the Brian's work parties, though. I even shave my legs and use that rub-on tan stuff. I only see Brian's work people two or three times a year, so I developed this alter ego for those parties. And my alter ego likes things flashy and trashy. The very first work party I went to, though, I was a nervous wreck. I didn't know anyone, so I couldn't just call up a veteran wife and be all 15 and stuff: "Like, hey! Are you going to that lame work thing? Yeah, what a drag. So, whacha wearing? Send me a pic and I'll wear something matching!"

The memo called for semi-formal attire. As far as I was concerned, jeans were semi-formal; with a nice sweater and some cute black heels, I had a good thing going on. However, Brian's business was somewhat conservative, and I'm certain that this is not what "The Firm" pictured when they said semi-formal. So a friend and I loaded up and went to the big city where we shopped at a Targets, which screams semi-formal to me. See, we don't have a Targets in my town, unfortunately. And a chance to shop there really makes me feel all kinds of fancy.

After two bags of popcorn and a white cherry Icee, we finally found a dress that we believed to be semi-formal and shoes to match. Still, I fretted about it well into the party when I realized (after a glass or five of white zinfandel) that I looked just as good, if not better than any other woman there. And even some of the men. The more white zin I had, the better I looked. Brian cut me off and dragged me home just before I began actually telling people just how good I looked.

When it was time to start shopping for the second party, I drank the white zinfandel before I went shopping and came out of the store with a cute little number made of gold and black shiny material. It said so on the tag: "100 percent shiny material; dry clean only." Again, I shaved my legs and rubbed on a tan and called myself flashy and trashy. Really trashy, if you must know the truth. It wasn't actually my fault I was so trashy; my dress was slightly too big, so it kept sliding down and exposing my bra strap. So, I excused myself, those amaretto sours just run right through me, and affixed my magnetic nametag to my bra strap. Keep in mind that I never claimed to be an engineer, and by the end of the night, my nametag was halfway down my bicep and sideways. But at least you couldn't see my bra strap. At least I had a bra strap. I'm certain some of the other wives were not partaking of any support. Again, Brian cut me off and took me home before I had a chance to point out their lack of support.

Yet again, Brian's Christmas party is coming up. There's a new leader at the helm, and he's declared that for this party dress will be "casual." I have no idea what's casual these days, much less what's stylish as well as casual.

When I dress casual, I have donut glaze on my sweatshirt because I woke up too late to unwrap the pop tarts, so I had to drive through. My socks don't match, and I have only one earring in because The Daughters have played in my jewelry drawer and I forgot to put the other earring in when I had to rinse and spit. My jeans have snot on the hip where a student gave me a hug (and wiped her nose) the day before, but they (the jeans) don't stink so I'm wearing them again. This is casual to me. I'm not sure Brian will escort me to the party looking like this, but I will have the trashy part of my flashy-trashy persona represented.

I have really got to make more friends in his circle so I can call someone up and at least borrow a blouse.

Actual Conversation With Daughter 1 As I'm Trying To Head Out The Door To A Very Important PTO Meeting Where We All Sign Up To Bring Cookies For The Class Party And No One Signs Up To Supervise.

(This also explains why I buy all of my clothes at the second-hand store.)

Daughter 1 (while coloring at the dining room table): Momma, you have something on your shirt.

Me: Nope. I just pulled this out of the laundry basket and it looks as clean as it smells. I doubled checked.

Daughter 1: No, Momma. You do have something on your shirt.

Me (looking down at my chest): I do? Where?

Daughter 1: Right there (uses red marker to make a mark on my shirt where no mark previously existed) on your breast.

Me: Honey! You just made that mark!

Daughter 1: No I didn't. It was there before. See, I had red and the mark was blue, like this. (Picks up blue marker and makes a new mark)

Me: Honey! Quit marking on my shirt!

Daughter 1: I'm not, Momma.

Me: Yes, you are. I just watched you make this red mark and this blue mark.

Daughter 1: You did?

Me: Yes.

Daughter 1: Then why didn't you move?

Momma Vs. the Professional

I turned to the Internet to find out how one would become a professional anything. I looked first at freecollegeclasses.org. No, I'm not lying, it's a website. Go ahead. Look it up. I'll wait.

Told ya.

According to that particular website, there are three steps that one needs to take to journey from amateur boxer to professional boxer:

1. Learn to fight,
2. Make a name for yourself,
3. Hire a manager and schedule your professional debut.

Simple enough, right?

To become a professional baker, you need to learn to bake, perfect your baking, and charge money for your baked goods.

To become a professional truck driver, you need to earn your truck driving license, be trained by a truck driving school, drive a truck and then learn to honk your horn at little girls in minivans who are pumping their little arms up and down in an L-formation. That specific information did not come from freecollegeclasses.org.

Nowhere, as you may have already guessed, is there a definitive answer as to how a momma breaks through to the professional ranks. I know there are Professional mommas Mothers (I do not take the use of the term "momma" lightly) out there. When I lament about not getting The Daughters to bed on time, they are the first to email me suggesting that I try the dozens of "proven sleep techniques" that I have already tried. They are sweet as potatoes and always end their suggestions in a backhanded fashion by saying something along the lines of, "Hang in there. Not everyone has a knack for this kind of thing."

"This kind of thing," however is the oldest profession. Okay, maybe the next to the oldest profession. And, despite the Casey Anthonys and the Octomoms of the world, I believe that every woman has a knack for it somewhere in her being. My knack, I will be the first to admit, is buried beneath an ice cream-inspired bulge on my thighs.

I will also admit that I used to aspire to be a Professional Mother. I read the Nazi-esque book about waking your newborn baby every two hours in the night to feed her. This way, you can establish your authority as a parent by securing a schedule you can live with. For starters: Waking every two hours throughout the night is not a schedule I can live with. And, if I honestly feel the need to establish my authority over a newborn baby, my troubles are thicker than Schwarzenegger's accent. (Yes, I know he was Austrian and not German. I was in the European neighborhood, though.)

I remember swaying a screaming Daughter 2 as I stood in the fifteen-person deep express line at Hellmart waiting to purchase a box of condoms when one mother interjected that I should be shushing my child as well as swaying her. "She's used to being in your ever-rocking and swaying womb with your heart beat as her own personal stereo system." I wanted to travel back in time and give her father a condom. Wouldn't a sympathetic grin have been sufficient? Wouldn't it have just been kinder for her to have said, "Bless your heart"? Would it have killed her to buy me a chocolate bar?

Besides, I completely relate to my child, every time I'm in line at Hellmart, I feel like pitching a little fit as well myself.

When you become a Professional Mother, does the pay increase? And by that, I mean do you start finding paper money in the dryer instead of the seventeen random cents that rattle through the fluff cycle of a dryer full of towels?

When you become a Professional Mother, do you have to be tested for juicing before taking your children to birthday parties and swim lessons and, God-forbid, Chuck E. Cheese? If that happens, I will never attain professional status. Momma needs her juice to face the pizza-pushing rodent.

Do Professional Mothers get an off-season? Is there a certain time of the year when they get to go away with just a trainer for a while? Then they return to their families knowing all the latest blocking techniques and the best position to score. I wouldn't mind some momma-only time, but I'm sure as hell not training for anything.

Will I become a professional when I have folded 31,998 loads of laundry? Will I reach pro status when I fix 1,274 home cooked meals in a row? Will I be considered the mother of all mothers when I successfully have my children bathed, clothed and to school on time for 11,121 days in a row? Those are awfully high bars.

And I prefer to keep my bars set low. And dark. And with a bartender who knows how much grenadine to add to a whiskey sour to make it just right.

I guess what I'm getting at is that I'm really and truly comfortable with my amateur status. I don't want to have to exert all my knowledge upon poor, unkempt, unslept souls who wander the grocery store aisles with their carts flowing over with grape jelly and peanut butter. I don't want to become the authority on the best way to sneak spinach and squash into my picky eater's diet. I actually kind of like serving chicken nuggets and sliced cheese five nights a week. That, right there, is a stress reliever like no other.

Most of all, I don't want to be the authoritative mother that the professionals seem to be. If I had adhered to every single piece of advice I'd ever received from well-meaning professional mothers, my poor babies would have grown up as orphans, their mother having been institutionalize with a nervous breakdown over not securing the Huxtable lifestyle in my dirty-undies-on-the-kitchen-floor home.

I'm happily content with my amateur status. It provides my family with laughs we never dreamed possible, meals we never conceived cookable and a life that is truly worth living. Plus, it gives me an excuse to drink an entire bottle of sangria before bed each and every night. I'm kidding. It's just a half-bottle.

Acknowledgments

My Pulitzer Prize Acceptance Speech ... For This Year

I really do have the best family around. It started with my parents, Harriett and Rowland Smith, who allowed me to be silly. Really, it was just my own momma who allowed me to be silly. My daddy told me countless times to quit fiddle-fartin' around. My sister, Rachel, allowed me to pick on her relentlessly. And by allowed, I mean I was older and bigger, and she could do nothing to stop me.

I met the best man in the world, and convinced him he couldn't live without me. He pushes me to write more and write better and to just write. He loves me and encourages me and smiles when I overshare fun facts about him. Like how he reads *Cosmo* in the bathroom. Gah, I sure do love that man.

I have two of the most amazing, most beautiful, most crazy daughters that have ever walked this earth. They are my first editors. ("Momma, don't blog about that. BUT, if you wanna tell about the time I farted during dinner, I approve.") Thank you. I don't need their approval, but I want it and value it. I love them more and more.

My bestie, FloJo, whose real name is Heather Sheffield, sat down with the very rough first draft of this book and spent several days at Starbucks going over it with colored pens, highlighters and Post-Its. For taking the time away from her family to chill with my book at Starbucks, you're welcome. Um. I mean thank you. Plus, she let me write about our antics. Correction: Some of our antics. I couldn't ask for a better friend.

There is a fabulous group of Mommas who have been oversharing my life for a very long time. They read the very first, very rough draft. Muche Inman, Shelley Ullrich, Tiffany Chona, and Kathleen Johnson: Thanks for honestly laughing with me and not at me. I appreciate your friendship more than I appreciate a late-morning snooze.

I have an amazing critique group who got out their fine-tooth combs and whipped through this book with honesty—thank you for your summer. I will cheer for your anatomy anytime. "Go TITS!"

My editor, Mari Farthing, is nothing short of awesome. It all started with a tweet, "Wanna do lunch?" I said yes and the rest is girl-crush history. [Note from my editor: Mutual girl crush, for the record.] My publisher, Buzz Books USA, and specifically Malena Lott, is a great ball of fire. I am so glad she said yes to me and this oversharing venture.

And finally, to my readers: You keep laughing … I'll keep sharing. Thank you.

Thank you.

Thank you.

About the Author

Heather Davis has a finely tuned snarky side, which she uses on a daily basis to save her sanity. She is married to a very patient husband, and together they have two very entertaining daughters. *Oversharing My Life*, a collection of humorous essays, is her debut book.
She and her family live in Bartlesville, OK, where she chronicles her life at www.Minivan-Momma.com.

Also by Heather Davis
TMI Mom Bites the Big Apple (humorous travel essays, ebook exclusive)

Coming late Fall 2013: *Fooling Around,* TMI Mom Book 2

You may also enjoy these titles from Buzz Books:

Next Left by Dani Stone, an ebook novelette, fiction
Something New by Malena Lott, trade paperback and ebook, fiction
Dance Mom Survival Guide by Malena Lott and Jill Martin, trade paperback and ebook

For the full list of titles and to get to know our authors, visit www.BuzzBooksUSA.com.

18232677R00152

Made in the USA
Charleston, SC
23 March 2013